Portrait of John Paul II

ANDRÉ FROSSARD
of the French Academy

Portrait of John Paul II

Translated by
Mary Emily Hamilton

IGNATIUS PRESS SAN FRANCISCO

Title of the French original:
Portrait de Jean-Paul II

Cover design by Riz Boncan Marsella
Cover photo by Joe Rimkus, Jr.,
Catholic News Service

ISBN 0–89870–277–1
Library of Congress catalogue number 89–83259
Printed in the United States of America

Contents

This book is not a biography and makes no attempt to furnish a chronology of the acts of the Holy Father's pontificate (a mere listing would require more than a hundred pages): it is a portrait. As such, any inadequacies therein are the responsibility of the portrait-painter, not of the model.

The stove used to make the smoke which announces the outcome of papal elections.

Prologue:

Habemus Papam! *We Have a Pope!*

On October 16, 1978, toward the end of the afternoon, the chimney on the roof of the Sistine Chapel began to emit white smoke from the stove within, but no one yet knew that that soft smoke was to have the impact of a cannonball: it would break the chain of Italian popes with the election to that supreme office of the first Slav in history, a man whom the conclave, in a stroke as bold as it was unexpected, called forth from behind the Iron Curtain.

Those who were standing close to the newly elected Pope when he first heard the news said that for a moment he went perfectly still, and his face turned as white as a dead man's.

But after he had accepted the office and announced that he would take the name John Paul II, and after they took him into the sacristy of the Sistine Chapel and dressed him in the white cassock, one would have thought he had always been Pope.

Paris:

An Invitation to Represent France at the Coronation

I was not expecting to go to Rome. An unfamiliar voice on the telephone, calling from the Élysée Palace, informed me that the President was sending me to represent France at the new Pope's coronation, along with Prime Minister M. Raymond Barre, Secretary of State Alain Peyrefitte, and a young priest of Polish extraction from the north of France. I had met M. Giscard d'Estaing only once, in the corner office in the Faubourg Saint-Honoré where he was kind enough, one day, to explain his political position to me so that I would get it right when I wrote about him. He did not say anything afterward, so I thought I must have made a good impression, but I had no idea it was *that* good.

My wife was in the hospital, where she was enjoying her convalescence following a delicate knee operation (she is not afraid at all of hospitalization, but on the contrary looks forward to it the way most people look forward to vacations). That, at least, gave me a plausible excuse to put off responding to the invitation for an hour or so—until I could verify the call. It turned out to be the real thing, and my wife was very understanding and willing for me to go. I was off duty, so at the appointed time I found myself standing on the tarmac at Villacoublay, ready to board the government airplane. These little military planes look very nice on the outside. Inside, however, there are few amenities. I sat behind the government ministers, with my knees pushed up against my chin, and jackknifed into this unnatural posture I overheard, thanks to a brief interval when the engines were relatively quiet, M. Raymond Barre confiding to his secretary of state that he had "never been too crazy about Solzhenitsyn". At the time, people were still going on about Solzhenitsyn as if he were some sort of "little David of the Gulag" who had just hit the Soviet Goliath right between the eyes, employing as the lethal stone in his slingshot a short book called *One Day in the Life of Ivan Denisovich.* The giant still looked quite fearsome, but his brains were beginning to leak out of the hole in his skull and dissidents were streaming from the Soviet Union all over Europe. I cannot fathom why the furor over Solzhenitsyn failed to breach our prime minister's defenses, and I guess I'll never know: immediately afterward, the plane started bucketing in an air pocket like a motorboat in the wake of a steamship and we were on the ground before I heard another word.

Rome:

Breaking with Tradition

There's a lot to be said for being a government VIP, even if you only get to be one for a day or two. Your suitcases reach your destination without any effort on your part, doors open by themselves, policemen are on the scene only to clear obstacles from your path. Preceded by a fine motorcycle escort, who, splendid in blue uniforms and white gloves, rode effortlessly along without holding onto the handlebars so as to wave traffic aside on our left and on our right, I don't believe it took us more than ten minutes to go from Ciampino Military Airport, south of Rome, to the Villa Bonaparte, our embassy at the other end of the city. The Villa Bonaparte, a big, unimposing residence but for its elegant interior and furnishings, sits at the entrance to vast gardens that are the envy of the other members of the diplomatic corps. Inside, you walk on gorgeous marble floors, even on the extremely rare yellow Siena marble that convinces your feet that they are gliding on rivulets of honey. The ambassador had invited a few extra guests to keep the government ministers company, since government ministers are universally reputed to be incapable of amusing themselves. Nobody had met the new Pope. A few people had heard Karol Wojtyla mentioned in conversation, and one prelate remembered that he was the one who had spoken up several times at the Second Vatican Council (in fact, he spoke sixty times), during the debate on the Constitution *Gaudium et spes*.

What was sensational was this break in the long procession of Italian popes. Everybody was talking about the conclave's daring initiative, the Curia's astonishment at who was going to be their new Pope and the new Pope's equivalent wonder at who would compose his Curia, where mysteries of faith maintain offices of their own.

But nobody could have imagined what was about to happen the next day, when a way of practicing Christianity that some people thought as good as dead, passé, sociologically irrelevant, extant only in murals on walls of empty Vatican apartments, would burst in to reassert itself among us.

The first appearance of Pope John Paul II.

Saint Peter's:

Meeting the New Pope (Almost)

Those who were there that day will never forget it.

The crowd, squeezed in the pincers of Saint Peter's Square, spilling out in a multicolored torrent almost all the way to the banks of the Tiber, was expecting to see a pope, but without warning found itself in the presence of a fisher of men, in every respect the equal of those Christ called to himself on the shores of the Sea of Tiberias. One might have said that the newcomer could not have journeyed from Poland but instead had arrived from Galilee, with a fishing net slung over his shoulder and the book of the Gospels under his arm, and that from somewhere under the basilica a hidden time warp had made void the sweep of years between his coming and Saint Peter's burial in the tomb beneath the great church.

I have often described my first impression: Nero's circus rose through the marble floors of Saint Peter's, history abruptly took a sharp turn from the horizontal to the vertical. The man in the white cassock whom we saw before us looked like one of the original apostles, and his very first words, "Fear not!", uttered in a tone that seemed to set all the bells in Rome ringing, called us to witness that here indeed stood an authentic apostle. One would have said that their sound was gone out from the entrance to the Colosseum, that these were the days of persecution come back all over again, with a pope advancing from the catacombs, beckoning the faithful to follow him into the very mouths of the lions. The crowd behind the police barriers in the square did not know what to do; people's curled index fingers furtively wiped the lower lids of their obviously misty eyes. The ambassadors standing beside me had tears in their eyes too: I don't know if anyone has ever seen diplomats openly weeping while on official business; only rarely has such a phenomenon been ascribed to the weather. I was crying myself, along with everyone else, without being at all clear about the reason why. I felt as if I were privileged to be present at a once-in-a-lifetime event: we were together seeing God working his purpose out in a moment of human history, an apprehension all too infrequent and all too often missed.

John Paul II was crowned without a crown. The three-tiered crowns, that for some symbolize the different powers of the papacy and for others the Church Militant, the Church Suffering, and the Church Triumphant, are lined up in glass cases in the sacristy of the Sistine Chapel, as one enters through a door cut under the base of the *Last Judgment*. Missing is the one shaped like a sparkling, hand-chased mortar shell that the Milanese gave to Paul VI, their former archbishop; he had to sell it to help the starving poor in India. Certainly the most beautiful and valuable piece in the collection is an exquisite triple crown fashioned of thin gold paper, the same kind used to wrap chocolates, that was made in Milan in the days when Napoleon Bonaparte had confiscated all the gold Milan possessed.

The new Pope wore a miter, a headdress like a bird's beak opened wide to catch the manna falling down from heaven; he held a staff before him that was surmounted by a long, slender crucifix. With his white cassock sculpted to his body by the wind, he resembled the statues on top of the colonnade. He was thirty or forty paces away; I hoped to get a closer view of him the next day at the audience he was going to give for the official delegates. At that audience, there would be only two hundred of us instead of three hundred thousand, and perhaps then I would be able to explain successfully to myself why we had received this Pope with tears of gratitude before he had even done anything, and why we had had, from the minute he took his first steps toward us, the feeling that all our sins were forgiven.

The audience was set for eleven o'clock in the morning, and the delegates circumspectly arranged themselves behind the representatives of the Republic of Andorra, whose privileged position, confirmed by alphabetical order, always entitles them to a place in the front row at official functions. John Paul II arrived at noon and crossed the room with long strides, leading a line of monsignori who huffed and puffed trying to keep up with him. He stepped onto the platform, spoke for a moment with the heads of some of the delegations, notably with M. Raymond Barre, and then left, so to speak, without ever getting off his horse. All I can remember of his passing among us is a broad wake of billowing white wool and a face with a friendly, slightly mischievous smile.

However, I shelved my disappointment for another day. The cardinals were to meet with the Pope the next afternoon, and my two government ministers, having been called back to Paris, entrusted the Republic half to me and half to the outstanding Polish priest who had discreetly remained with us ever since we had left Paris. This gave me an excellent chance at last to get close to the unusual man who had moved the crowd so profoundly with those two words "Fear not!" that are found so often in the Bible that no one takes much notice of them any more.

The reception was to be held in a hall with walls decorated

in marble carved to represent curtains raised above a stage, a baroque device that I saw as an attempt to convince us all that Christianity had ceased to be something new but had become more like a play that would never see its final curtain. Unfortunately, as soon as I entered the room, I was overcome by a familiar dizzy feeling that I could not shake off. They brought me a velvet chair, sympathetic ladies clustered around me trying to be of help. The room rolled to port and to starboard like a ghost ship in a fog. On the bridge of the phantom vessel I saw some of the red-robed cardinals who already had their sea legs chatting with other personages dressed in black, heedless of the continual pitching and tossing.

I would have been happier had I felt a little better as I prepared to greet the Holy Father. But he had been delayed, so seriously delayed that he never got there, so he sent his apologies. Eventually, my vertigo subsided enough for me to approach a few charitable souls to tell them how sorry I was that I had not been able, in three days of trying, to get near the Holy Father. They listened graciously, but I realized my words were in vain; I wasn't going to get to meet the Pope.

That same evening, I started for Paris with the good priest who had wept with us in the square. We were both in a reflective mood. Two hundred forty-six popes had succeeded Saint Peter, and if their deaths evoked a certain amount of emotion among the faithful, as if a litany in a liturgical office had been interrupted all of a sudden in the middle of a versicle, their elections always brought rejoicing. The work of prayer, suspended for a brief time, resumed its accustomed round for the comfort of the individual Christian and in the interest of the proper ordering of the religious history that the Church patiently writes over the lines set down by secular historians.

Paul VI had gone gently, at the end of his strength. One of his last public statements had been an outcry of indignation and horror at the violence and cruelty in a world that seemed to be going back to barbaric times, and it seemed a wonder that such a fine, cultivated person, hurled by circumstances beyond his control into an era of political insanity where terrorism, in his own country, most often acted out its hatred of power by killing the very people who knew how to be careful in exercising authority, had not died long ago of a broken heart. His worn-out, thin body had lain in state for some time on the steps of Saint Peter's, when it had to be replaced, to everyone's consternation, by that of his successor John Paul I, a sweet, good man, whom nobody had ever suspected of being in delicate health until they found him dead in his bed one morning after a reign of only a month. This premature death immediately aroused speculation on the part of certain suspicious types who never take anything at face value, who doubt that anything ever takes its natural course at the Vatican, and who see the ghosts of the Borgias hovering in every alcove, planning and plotting even now. We had grieved for these two popes. What was unusual was that we had wept also when we got a new one. The young priest sitting across from me in the jump seat facing backward in the plane could not plumb the mystery either, and without having come to any sort of satisfactory conclusion we found ourselves landing in the fog.

Paris:

Just Who Is Karol Wojtyla, and What Is He Going to Do?

In the airport lobby we were still asking each other questions and wondering about the answers. At the moment when John Paul II slipped the Fisherman's Ring onto his finger, the state of the one, holy, catholic and apostolic Church could not have been said to have been at its most flourishing. Of course, the Holy Roman Church had always been catholic and always would be, but subtle minds with questionable motives were calling all her dogmas to question one after another. These individuals, wise as serpents but by no means harmless as doves, chose not to attack the Church's teachings head-on but mounted an insidious campaign to drain them of their content by making each of them a basis for what they called a "problematic". The Church still was and always would be apostolic, but a French bishop showed himself unwilling to assert that bishops "possess the fullness of truth", with the result that his crosier became a pure symbol of doctrinal confusion, missionaries maintained that their mission was not to announce the good news but "to be open", and finally the apostle who had renounced his real mission put on a helmet, not of salvation but of revolution. The Church still was and always would be Roman, but Rome's Magisterial instructions, conveniently abridged, appeared or rather disappeared on page 27 of any given Catholic newspaper, the sternest warnings of the Holy See started to be taken as mere suggestions, and it was now chic to receive a papal reprimand as if it were a compliment.

To the disinterested observer, the Church was showing clear signs of internal disintegration. There were at least two Churches in Holland: one of them was playing at throwing its hat over the blades of the windmill and then attempting to catch it as it flew off on the other side; the other Church of Holland, the conservative one, called "anachronistic" and "reactionary", kept constantly on the defensive, even had its communications cut off by the windmill faction. In Germany, there was a theologian who persisted in calling himself a Catholic while inveighing against Rome in the manner of a Luther, but with rather less eloquence and rather more pedantry. In Spain, always very Catholic, the higher clergy let themselves float on the prevailing winds. In France, we watched the first punches thrown in the boxing match between an ultraconservative bishop so obsessed with the old liturgical formulas that he came close to branding the Second Vatican Council a work of the devil and an opposing clerical contingent manifestly ready to throw the liturgical and pastoral baby out with the bathwater, clergy who continually preached democracy and pluralism only to take refuge in their own divinely conferred rights every time they thought their authority was being questioned. This group, so easily led around by the nose that it was incredible, took the slightest objection as an insult and the meekest question as evidence of intolerable defiance. In the United States, some of the clergy who were persuaded that the best way to combat error is to appear to partake of it yourself, meddled in every conflict in contemporary society and fabricated a pastoral approach to homosexuality over the ruins of Christian marriage. In Latin America, the "popular churches" drew themselves up in full battle array against the institutional Church, all the while insisting, of course, that they were doing nothing of the sort. And I must not leave out Central America, where the superior of a contemplative order had all his monks psychoanalyzed and thereby emptied his monastery. He himself was the first to leave, so he could tie the knot with his girlfriend, who was entirely too young to get married in the first place—assuming it would palliate my shock if he explained to me in advance that I really knew nothing about the contemplative life. Deprived of sound catechetical instruction, disoriented by theologians who instead of providing clear and distinct norms praised "the courage to doubt", Christians no longer knew what they ought or ought not to believe, and they suffered all the more in the silent stampede as the faithful deserted the churches and attendance steadily declined.

Now here came this Pope. He stood in the doors of the basilica and as soon as he did, my young traveling companion and I, and thousands more besides, had not only the comforting feeling of awakening from a bad dream, but the deeper, stranger, rarer impression of having been touched by grace.

But just who *was* he?

Paris:

Another Chance for an Audience

Every day requests for private or group audiences pour into Rome, and I was not at all certain that my own—that besides had never been put in writing—would ever be remembered. Then, one fine morning some weeks after the coronation without a crown, a short note enclosed in an ordinary envelope from John Paul II's Polish secretary informed me as if it were the most normal thing in the world that if I ever had occasion to come to Rome again, the Pope would be glad to receive me. Could some one of the kind folks I had talked to when I was feeling dizzy have obtained this favor for me? I still don't know.

As for that "occasion", it presented itself almost simultaneously with the letter's arrival: six thousand European students who were having a convention in Rome invited me to give the closing address at their meeting. I bless these young people whose generous thoughtfulness accorded so well with my fondest wishes. They told me, in addition, that an audience with John Paul II would follow the closing of the convention. Good news, like bad news, always comes in batches. My wife and I boarded the airplane. It was not that same little white government plane, and there would be no white-gloved carabinieri to greet us when we got off. But this time I would probably get a bit closer to this Pope people were already talking about a great deal, and to whom were being attributed various "charisms"—a word church people had brought into vogue only recently, just since they had decided to speak Greek in preference to Latin, the better to be understood.

Rome:

A Papal Welcome, and The Surprise of My Life

My European students joyfully convened, displaying that exuberance that proceeds from clear consciences and sound morality, when that morality is drawn from God's wisdom and not from human wisdom, for human wisdom never brought happiness to anyone. As soon as they had explained to me why they had held their convention and what they had accomplished, I made them a nice closing speech. Then the whole crowd trooped across Rome and invaded the *aula*, the new building constructed especially for papal audiences; it looks like a gigantic ear all lighted up. At the rear it has a throne, and above the throne a depiction of Christ rising obliquely from a sort of Burning Bush worked in gilded bronze.

As soon as he came in the Pope was welcomed with deafening applause, like six thousand flags flapping in the breeze. The clapping in unison lasted more than five minutes. The Pope sat patiently on his throne, patting his foot in time to the beat. When the tumultuous ovation finally died down enough for him to begin, the theme he had chosen made my jaw drop: it was "Penance". What a subject, so soon after those days in May of 1968 when the students had rioted to claim everything else *but* the right to go to confession; was this not going to provoke them? The professors in the front seats turned around to look at the audience with what seemed to me a sort of nervous curiosity, but they need not have worried. The assembly had passed through exhilaration into enthusiasm, and they cheered for penance without even waiting to hear about absolution. This Pope, who can make young people of twenty applaud a sacrament that has a hard time getting to be everyone's favorite (I said to myself), is not done amazing us yet.

When the Pope had finished speaking, the audience's expression of warmth was even more bountiful than it had been at the beginning. The professors, their wives, and the rest of us were led into a small reception room adjoining the *aula*, where the Pope, they told us, would come to meet us. Indeed he did, and he spoke a few kind words to each person present. My wife asked for his prayers, and since everyone had to say something to him, I said, alluding to the applause that had not yet ceased to echo from the other side of the wall: "Holy Father, you will lead these young people where you want them to go." He answered simply, "I hope so", and went out.

"Well," I thought to myself, "that's the end of my audience with the Pope." I was about to leave the hall when the prefect of the palace, Monsignor Martin, and the Pope's secretary strode rapidly up to me and whispered in my ear: "Be at the Bronze Door at a quarter to seven tomorrow morning. You are to attend the Holy Father's Mass and have breakfast with him afterward." Not in living memory among Vatican watchers of that day had such an extraordinary invitation been bestowed more than once, and the beneficiary that time had been none other than King Baudouin. Since then, a number of people have been invited to John Paul II's private chapel. He has been the most welcoming and approachable Pope in history. But up to that point, such a thing was still unheard of.

My initial astonishment promptly gave way to anxiety about oversleeping and arriving late, a worry that beset me all evening. I set my alarm for five o'clock in the morning, and I informed the hotel porter that he should be sure to knock on my door at that time as well. As an added precaution, I asked the late Father-General of the Norbertines, dear Monsignor Calmels, whose recent death has saddened us: "What time do the Norbertines get up?" "At five o'clock", he told me, and he agreed to telephone me as soon as he was up. I still had to arrange how I was going to get there. I had rented a car, since I so enjoy driving in Rome where motoring, the natives say, "is more a matter of opportunity than of vehicle codes". But cars can fail to start, cars can break down, so I ordered a taxi for six o'clock in the morning, and in the event the taxi did not come on time, I asked an old friend to stop by and pick me up at that same early hour. The Vatican was only a ten-minute drive from the hotel, but I had to be sure to be ready in time to walk it if all mechanical means of transportation fell short. I had done my best to insure against every conceivable foulup, but for all that, I still did not feel easy in my mind. And with good reason. My alarm clock, stamped "Made in Japan", spoke American English. In fine print it indicated the hours *ante meridiem* and the hours *post meridiem*, so that what I thought said a.m. really said p.m.: the alarm went off at five in the afternoon. The dear Norbertine really did telephone me at the hour we had agreed on, but the hotel porter had taken his receiver off the hook in order not to be disturbed. If I had gone to sleep, I would never have been up on time; as it was, I hardly slept at all, and never more than fifteen minutes at once. My old friend came to give me a ride and so did the taxi driver, whom I paid for his trouble and sent on his way. We got to the Vatican at ten after six.

The sun was not yet over the horizon, and Saint Peter's

The Swiss Guards of the Vatican.

looked like a chalk sketch on carbon paper. Bernini's magnificent colonnade, whose innumerable shafts serve only to support their architect's reputation, was deserted. We walked the hundred paces around it, exchanging opinions that had more sleep than sense in them, concerning the development of the papacy since Julius II. At twenty minutes before seven, the Bronze Door, at the top of a flight of steps at the farther end of the colonnade, opened a crack; a Swiss Guard poked his nose out and scrutinized me, frowning. Of course, he didn't believe a word of what I said to him. They had not yet grown used to receiving the Pope's visitors so early in the morning. The nose disappeared and then popped back out. I stated my name and business again. Another Swiss Guard, seated behind a small desk in the gallery that leads to Bramante's peculiar staircase whose design distorts perspective, consulted his lists, looked surprised and motioned the other Swiss Guard to let me in. I left my good old friend and went from Swiss Guard to Swiss Guard until I arrived at Saint Damasus' Court, empty as it almost always is; then I entered another, much smaller court, where daybreak cast a shaft of light. There were no more Swiss Guards, but there was a porter and a smiling nun who was so self-effacing that it seemed she might fade back into the woodwork at any moment. A tiny elevator took us up to the third floor of the papal palace (really the fourth floor), familiar to pilgrims as the one where the pope appears at the time of the Angelus.

In the chapel furnished by Paul VI in the private apartments, the Pope was already at prayer. He always kneels near the entrance before he goes to his bronze prie-dieu, an imposing piece of furniture equipped with a large desktop for writing, where the Pope really does write occasionally in the presence of the Blessed Sacrament, just as he used to do in his chapel in Cracow, where he did his work behind double-locked doors at a small desk placed where he could see the altar. Every morning, on this prie-dieu, he finds the copious lists of Mass Intentions neatly stacked by a nun of the order whose duty it is to care for the papal apartments.

One day later on, he was to tell me, "When I was young, I kept thinking prayer ought not to consist of anything but praise or thanksgiving. The 'Prayer of Petition' seemed to me to be utterly unworthy. But as I got older, I changed my mind. Today, I ask for a lot and I beg for still more grace for that little nun and her wad of Mass Intentions."

Two prie-dieux upholstered in gray velvet had been placed behind the Holy Father's; only then did it occur to me that I was going to have a hard job explaining to my wife how I had failed to realize that she too had been expected to share in all this.

The Pope says Mass slowly and very beautifully. His two secretaries serve as his acolytes and help him on with his vestments before he goes to the altar, and this ordinary ritual takes on a sacramental complexion. He pays such careful attention to his gestures, he pronounces the words of the Liturgy with such intensity, that as he celebrates the Mass he opens a new dimension in the minds of everyone present. While the city outside revolves all day like a merry-go-round whose riders may be power hungry, or handicapped, or dreamers, or destitute street people, the essential thing is that from this rock that is the cornerstone of all the rest of the day's work, this re-presentation each morning of Christ's Passion, whether celebrated by the Pope or by the humblest priest in the silence of a clinic, flows a living fountain for the life of a world that no longer understands how all life proceeds from spirit, a truth well known to the men who wrote the Creed ("the Holy Spirit, the Lord and Giver of Life"), but a truth too long ignored that no doubt physics will soon rediscover, and a truth that must be staff and stay for human hopes that our theologies and watered-down philosophies are no longer in any condition to support.

Although there was no homily, something that for once we regretted, the Mass, which may be said in whatever languages the Pope chooses to accommodate his guests of various nationalities, lasted about fifty minutes and seemed short at that. It was followed by a time of thanksgiving, a devotional exercise that has fallen into disuse in Western countries where it has become customary for people to leave after Communion.

On that particular morning, the Pope rose from his prie-dieu about eight o'clock, took me kindly by the arm, and said: "And now, come, we will talk together a little."

We talked a lot.

At meals, the Pope sits by himself on one of the long sides of the table: this is all that remains of the time-honored protocol that decreed that a pope should have nothing in front of him but his water carafe or his wine from the Vatican's own grapevines. Guests sit across from him, and his two secretaries sit at the two ends of the table. His hard-working Polish secretary Don Stanislas Dziwisz, a young man with a calm demeanor and a brilliant, slightly ironic mind, is by nature a quiet person; but he knows all the right things to say and all the right times to say them, and he is always on his toes, ready for anything, like a cat about to jump out of a basket.

I was the Holy Father's only guest. We had just sat down when he began to question me about France, the way he questions a few laymen from every country he plans to visit. It is a habit, he tells me, that has always stood him in good stead. I told him that, as far as I had been able to determine, the national character of the French can be traced almost invariably to their Christian baptism; they are baptized very young, before they even have learned how to be French. I suspect they opted for Christianity, back in the days when they were still called Gauls, because they are sensitive to the workings of grace and to God's loving kindness to all men, to be sure, but further because of their taste for the radically different and their aversion to the Roman occupying forces who served as a ubiquitous symbol of imperial sway, forever reminding them that they were a conquered people, a subject nation. This peculiarity explains the French predilection for publicly opposing their government whenever they take a notion to, while it also explains why France has given the world so many moralists and so few metaphysicians, since metaphysics necessarily excludes any prior commitments, and the French are more committed in virtue of their baptism than they themselves even begin to understand. Traces of Christianity can be identified even in their anticlericalism or in the self-consciously subversive philosophy that motivated the French Revolution, a revolution Chesterton claimed was touched off by "Christian truths gone mad" (if it was not caused, as I myself am afraid, by straitjacketing those same Christian truths until they conformed to some people's definition of right reason). Julius Caesar had noticed early on that among the Gallic tribes there was an "elder brother party" and a "younger brother party", that is to say, a right wing preoccupied with holding on to what it had and a left wing necessarily determined to grab what it could.

The Holy Father listened to me with the courteous attention he gives to everyone. He is such a good listener that you even begin to get the impression you are saying something truly interesting. And all the while he was peacefully eating his bread and jam and scrambled eggs, I didn't take time to touch a thing unless it was my coffee cup—it must have been refilled at least ten times.

While I was on the subject, I thought I ought to make one

more point that would shed light on the French mentality. We French have always had a problem grasping the relationship between earthly things and heavenly things; it pains us when we are called on to reconcile them because we have it in our heads that they can hardly be made compatible with each other. While the Italians were rounding their arches and constructing domes that invited heaven's vault into their churches in a triumph of architectural hospitality, appropriately illuminated by a skylight, the French preferred perpendicular Gothic, building cathedrals ever higher to make sure all mankind could see how great a distance separates heaven from earth. Their Gothic style perpetuates, among other biases, the notion that divinity dwells beyond the reach of all but the man who stretches every fiber of soul and body to the limit. Now, *that* is where we get into morality. You can see the same attitude in French politics: they think there has to be some sort of ideal state, but that they will never be able to make such a state a reality. Their ideologues have erected many such Gothic theories, building of them spires that would fain climb high enough to touch the stars; fortunately wisdom, whose feet are always on the ground, is on duty here below to remind them that we cannot all be steeplejacks.

I didn't mention the Church in France to the Holy Father, and he didn't ask; that subject just never came up in any of our conversations.

Who ever would have thought he would ask me, at our very first meeting, to collaborate with him on a book? He had already learned how the media could distort anything he had to say. Some papers chose to summarize what he said and, in their hurry, missed his central point; others, not so innocently, edited out everything but what looked sensational enough to increase circulation or else cheerfully sliced and mutilated his texts in the manner of Jack the Ripper. A dialogue that we could create together would present his philosophy in a format that might stand a better chance of conveying his thought with some degree of accuracy, not to mention the advantage that a book penetrates further into the human consciousness and stays there longer than a picture or a scrap of information. And that was the reason he had invited me to breakfast.

In our book, he proposed we address the faithful in the simplest and most direct way we could. It was not supposed to be "an intellectual laboratory study", he said.

Popes never give interviews, but rather they express their thinking by using such different devices as the encyclical letter, the apostolic letter, the exhortation, the homily, the teaching, and I don't know how many others. But they never publish dialogues on their own initiative.

I was surprised. At first, I thought it was just an idea crossing the Holy Father's mind. Wrong. He had made a firm decision to do it.

I walked out of the papal apartments more bemused than I had been when I went in. I did not notice the porter in the little court or the Swiss Guards in the big one; I walked right past the staircase that goes down to the Bronze Door. Maybe all the coffee I had drunk had something to do with it, but more than anything else I was in the grip of a succession of emotions that I am not sure I have sorted out even now, ten years afterward. This Pope, who had never seen me before, had welcomed me as if he had known me for years, and our talk together had been perfectly relaxed, free of all those constraints and inhibitions that normally mark a one-to-one exchange between two people whose jobs have absolutely nothing in common and indeed are miles apart in responsibility. One of us, after all, had the whole weight of the

Church to bear, while I, on the other hand, had nothing heavier than my pen to lift.

Why had he invited me into his private world as if it were just the sort of thing he did every day, and why had he chosen to confide his most personal opinions to me, of all people? A French bishop, who had no better understanding than I did of why this Pope would not have preferred to work with a theologian, a philosopher—or indeed a French bishop, for instance!—later told me that I had been granted a privilege out of all proportion to my rank. I remained in ignorance of the answers to my two questions. When I finally came to myself enough to find the stairway leading to the exit, I stepped out into the secular world again, a world that issues many an invitation but is not nearly so gracious in receiving its guests.

Castel Gandolfo:

A Pilgrim Pope in France

The Pope had me come back to Rome or to Castel Gandolfo several times before he left on his visit to France. One evening, he sketched on the tablecloth with his fingernail the itinerary for his trip; he had more stops to make than a local commuter train. He was going to meet with many representatives of the clergy and a very few laymen, in private audiences, not to mention a sampling of members of parliament and representatives of ten or twelve Catholic Action groups, who would no doubt favor him with ten or twelve practically identical speeches on the problems of the modern world and what he, as pope, ought to do about them.

Since he had done me the honor of asking my opinion, I took the liberty of observing that France was a country where he would be welcomed not just by clergymen but by a great number of laymen, scientists, and philosophers who would be delighted to meet him, and whose ideas he might well find quite useful. He agreed, and juggled his schedule so as to leave a bit of time for them as well, asking me to bring him a list of about fifteen names by dawn the next day.

With the help of a couple of friends, both men of good will, I worked into the night deciding on fifteen men and women who would be the best ones to act as ambassadors of French thought. Of course we could think of more than fifteen, but choices had to be made, and I made them. This was the guest list for the "breakfast meeting with the intellectuals" that took place at seven one morning at the Papal Nuncio's residence in Paris. This small gathering of scientists, economists, and sociologists with the Pope caused some very hard feelings among those who did not get invited.

At Castel Gandolfo, a week or two after he returned from France, he told me that three "high points" of his tour stuck in his mind: his meeting with young people in the Parc des Princes (a stadium), his encounter with the enormous crowd in front of Saint Denis' Basilica, and the UNESCO reception where the assembly, composed of people from every culture on earth, applauded his speech on peace, the human family, and scientific cooperation so loudly and so frequently that he had to pause many times. Maybe it was this last that gave him the idea for the Assisi conference, where representatives of nearly every religion and spiritual persuasion in the world came together to discuss a simple idea: that it is both natural and good to believe in God, and that mankind would do well to remember that—right now, before it's too late. This multiracial meeting was denounced by right-wingers as a cop-out on the part of the Catholic Church that was supposed to be the "sole guardian of revealed truth". But in the very town where Saint Francis sang of Brother Wolf and Sister Grasshopper, could people not have a go at talking with Brother Moslem or Brother Buddhist without compromising their own Catholicism?

At Saint Denis', he formed an instantaneous rapport with the crowd made up of persons who did not live in Paris' best neighborhoods. They waited patiently, packed into the square elbow-to-elbow, as one hour stretched into two until the reverend gentlemen in the basilica deigned to release their prisoner. I think when he met the crowd in the square he perceived that Christianity has not disappeared from the

The Pope blesses a French teenager at Parc des Princes in Paris.

soul of the average man, as we have often been tempted to believe, but rather it still hangs on in human hearts at a level so deep that only the language of revelation can reach it and that consequently good pastoral care did not consist in reinjecting us with low doses of Christian religion dissolved in a huge bottle of sociopolitical intravenous solution. On the contrary, it was a matter of pumping the Faith out from the bedrock, where it has sunk down to hide, like undiscovered oil, beneath multiple layers of volcanic lava.

For decades our pastoral theology has been built on the notion that we have basically lost our first Faith. The work of John Paul II daily proved the opposite to be the case, and every one of his addresses to the peoples of the world possessed the singular ability to bring out again, more or less intact, that religious sense modern life has ostensibly deleted from rational minds. The Pope's visit to France must have brought about many conversions. For my own part, I could not forget those two young women who had never met before they were thrown together one evening in the midst of the noisy crowd and who felt the need to confess to me that they had just discovered both their Faith and their Church all over again, just as if they had come out into the daylight after a long journey in the shadows and found themselves back in their childhood homes.

In the Parc des Princes, the young people's warmth and his own were a perfect match for each other, and there was immediate mutual understanding. He treasures such a pleasant memory of this occasion that forever afterward he has always asked, before he takes a trip to a foreign place, "whether they have a Parc des Princes there". He spoke to the young people without watering down his language or sounding dictatorial either, he did not attempt to relax the requirements in the gospel, and they listened to him and understood him. We honor young people when we ask much of them, we demean them when we ask little. How disgusting are these graying adults who try so hard to look young that their pursuit of eternal youth amounts to idolatry, while they wouldn't dream of reminding young people not to abuse their state of grace while they still have those few fleeting years! Are they fooling anybody? In no way. Young people look with a mixture of wry amusement and revulsion at these old has-beens who can provide them with no more of a playing field than the shifting sands of their own complacency.

The Holy Father blamed himself then and still did months later for not answering the questions of a young man who, he said, was an atheist. The fellow had jumped up without warning and demanded, as if in a fever fit, to know such things as: "Why must one be a believer? What kind of God is this that you so adore?" The Pope kept trying humbly to find a reason for not having responded to him, and he did find one in the fact that he was caught up in the evening's tumult of enthusiasm. I was not qualified to grant him absolution, but I did have the credentials to conduct a modest inquiry that quite soon made it clear to me that this bold young atheist was really every bit as good a Christian as, if not a better Christian than, those apprehensive specialists in pastoral theology who had expressly forbidden spontaneous questions from the audience, thinking their forethought would serve to enliven the debate (although it did not lack anything in the way of liveliness), all the more because with his present-day questions, the young man was only asking the same things the twelve apostles must have had to listen to on every street corner in Jerusalem two thousand years ago.

Castel Gandolfo:

Fear Not! *Questions for the Pope*

It was then that the Holy Father hit upon the idea of a book in dialogue form, and while we were at lunch, he turned to me and said: "Ask me some questions."

I requested a few days' time to prepare them, and as soon as we got up from the table I headed for Ravenna by way of the road through the Apennines, a fine four-lane highway that suddenly narrows about thirty kilometers out of Cesena. At that point the thoroughfare snakes under a masterpiece of civil engineering that has been under construction for years and still shows no signs of nearing completion. I took advantage of the bottleneck to break my journey and visit Borgo San Sepolcro to see Piero della Francesca's *Resurrection*. His work has a dreamlike quality that makes the people in his paintings seem to glide through a silent realm beneath the sea: their eyes all have that look about them as if they were gazing out from eternity itself. Piero, who was a city alderman in Borgo San Sepolcro, painted his *Resurrection* on one of the walls of the old town hall that is now a municipal art gallery. It is a good-sized fresco, more than three meters by two. Christ is facing straight at you as he rises from the sepulcher, over the recumbent forms of the Roman soldiers, who do not look like they will be waking up any time soon. His cloak, draped over his left shoulder so that it leaves the right side of his upper body bare, is painted in that exquisite shade of pink that one sees in rosebuds. He still has one foot in the tomb, and his other foot, planted victoriously on the edge of the sarcophagus, looks massive enough to flatten everything and everybody. When the picture was painted, the city fathers were familiar with the contemporary notion that the glorified body is heavier than the mortal body and of sufficient density to exert a pull on the stars. His face has an awesome beauty depicted so as to show that he comes from another world, and his strangely fixed gaze seems to latch onto you, then look straight through you and zoom into outer space where it will drill holes in suns beyond our galaxy. This arresting painting effectively set the mood for the questions about the Faith that I intended to ask the Holy Father.

Ravenna:

Answers

Now a pope was about to vouchsafe his personal knowledge of the Faith to Christians throughout the world, and he was trusting me to convey his thought accurately. I felt a little frightened, as much because it was such an honor to be chosen to do this as because it would be hard to make certain I would be asking the questions my contemporaries would have asked had they been in my shoes. So I allowed the serene waves of the Adriatic to wash over my mind to cleanse and calm it, and in a few days I had composed five groups of questions on the Faith, the practice of that Faith, the Church, the world, and the persona of John Paul II, more precisely Karol Wojtyla. With each question I included the briefest possible statement of my reasons for asking it. When I finished, I found I had sixty-six questions to submit to the Pope—it seemed like a lot. But I thought he would probably throw out a certain number of them, maybe even half, and of course he would have questions of his own for me. Therefore I made a fair copy and retraced my route over the Apennine highway, not having enough time to detour to Monterchi to pray for help before the *Madonna del Parto*, whose intercessions I definitely could have used.

Back at Castel Gandolfo, the Holy Father asked me to give him two days to study my questionnaire. His decision surprised me: he was willing to answer all but one of my questions, the one having to do with an armed conflict that was going on at the time. He pointed out, with the good sense I must have been lacking when I asked it, that armies on the attack are not in the habit of coming to a dead halt right in front of an objective they intend to seize. But he let all the rest of the questions stand just as they were, set himself a work schedule, and since he was planning to answer all the questions that had to do with doctrine in Polish, he assigned an excellent sister on his staff to interpret for me. She not only had a Ph.D. in theology but was an accomplished Bible scholar besides, but she is one who would faint with horror if she saw her name mentioned in print. Her help was indispensable, and I don't know how I could have managed without her adeptness at deciphering the Holy Father's almost invisible marginal annotations that one might have thought he'd written with the point of a needle. A question mark above a line meant that the citation below it needed verification; if the question mark was below the line, it meant that the point deserved further discussion. The attempt on his life interrupted our work and prompted me to add a sixth chapter to give, in the face of so many conflicting and incorrect reports, an absolutely accurate account of the event. We had planned to devote a year to this book. It ended up taking two. As if it were the only thing the Pope had to do!

This was when I found out why it had been so easy to get my audience with the Holy Father at the beginning of his pontificate: in his series of answers to my questions on the Faith, he mentioned my book *Dieu existe, je L'ai rencontré,* that he had read in Cracow in its Polish translation and had enjoyed. Until this moment I had not known exactly what to say to people who asked why I had been converted at twenty in the Sisters' chapel on the Rue d'Ulm. Now I knew.

Castel Gandolfo:

The Papist and the Sportsman

The library at Castel Gandolfo has a huge window with long, sheer curtains that looks straight down on Lake Albano, where people paddling around in rented boats lazily soak up the sunshine. We didn't hear the Pope come in (he can steal up as quietly as a wolf), so when he said hello to my wife and me it gave us quite a start. He joined us for a moment to look out at the distant view of all the small craft silently weaving their way to and fro on the water.

"You know, I too used to be quite a sportsman", he said.

Maybe in some other life. Before he became the prisoner of these marble fastnesses. Today, if he were to go down there, rent himself a boat, and go rowing, the lake would become so crowded with boats filled with people wanting to see him that the crush would cause the same number of sinkings as a naval battle.

My wife excused herself to go for a walk. We sat down at one end of his big work table to go over a chapter of our book. When one particular sentence showed itself all too revelatory of my admiration for him, he immediately said, "You're too much of a papist. If I've told you that once, I've told you twenty times."

"Holy Father," I answered, "I'm not the only one. There are hundreds of millions of people just like me."

"That's no excuse."

"But anyhow, that's not what we're talking about here."

"Well, so much the better."

Rome:

John Paul II, Pontiff and Humorist

After lunch, we were walking around in the hall, and the Pope, who was in a jovial mood, told me a funny story, called in Italian a *barzelletta*:

The Pope was praying, and he asked God: "Lord, will Poland regain her freedom and independence some day?" "Yes," said God, "but not in your lifetime."

Then the Pope asked: "Lord, after I'm gone, will there be another Polish pope?" "Not in my lifetime", said God.

Paris:

The Perils of Being Polish

At first, the Pope used to read newspapers, at least some newspapers, but he soon tired of their monotonous harping. The same themes went 'round and 'round like a silly song with ninety-nine verses; most frequently the papers rearranged and replayed the old refrain from the *Lettres Persanes*, "How could anyone *possibly* be Polish?" with endless variations in every conceivable key.

You are allowed to be a German, a Chinese, or even a Patagonian if you cannot help yourself, but don't be Polish. That would be the wrong thing to do—you'd be a marked man. At a fancy dinner party in the city, a monk who moved in the highest social circles but was evidently somewhat hard of hearing said rather too loudly to his dinner partner, who had just told him how much she admired John Paul II: "Ah, Madame, it's true, he *is* Polish, but not to worry, he'll get over it." It was not unlike the headmaster in the British public school, reassuring a nervous mother: "Madam, your boy's having a hard go of it, to be sure, but with careful private tutoring he should be able to keep from having to repeat the Sixth Form."

The idea that there still may be some Poles left is a great comfort to Western minds, who look down, with a sense of self-satisfied superiority, on the benighted inhabitants of that obscure country who have not the opportunity to benefit from the latest trends in today's religious thought, those influential currents that spring from doubt and blend in so charmingly with the new age.

The election to the papacy of a Slav, born in Poland, a nation that learned her Christianity in both schools, Rome's and Byzantium's, that very Poland situated (that is, when the countries on both sides of her haven't either erased her boundaries completely or made her move to another longitude) at the point where the Orthodox Church and all the other Christian churches converge and where communism and democracy meet head-on, has been greeted as a kind of miracle of the Holy Spirit that gives Saint Peter a successor in the very best possible position to sort out conflicts and pave the way toward reconciliation in our contemporary world, and it has been taken as proof besides that Providence has not given up on his plan for us wretched human beings. Western intellectuals, who never admire anything but themselves for very long, have had therefore to think again. But not the simple folk. In his office in Saint Peter's Square, an excellent Spanish theologian elucidated this point for me with a charming illustration:

> The ordinary faithful are often more acutely sensitive to signs than we theologians are. If the lady of the house coughs at the dinner table, her dinner guests may think she has a cold. But her child, sitting at the foot of the table, knows right away that this is her signal to him that he has picked up the wrong fork. Now, the child is the common people; he is quicker than we are to heed signals, even if we are better than he is at explaining them. His mother means everything to him, and so the child seeks in her eyes what we have been combing our books to find.

Like all his fellow Poles, this Pope has lived under two totalitarian governments, and one of those two has until recently been crushing Poland under its enormous weight. If he were Greek, he might speak out against Turkish tyranny; if South American, against the Spanish conquistadors' oppression of the Indians; if he were a Black from South Africa, he might thunder against apartheid; he could base his speech either on his own experience or on that of his ancestors. But a Pole, given that he believes in God, would not speak out about religion or about Poland, because he is Polish and knows what reprisals might result. He cannot discuss Marxism-Leninism either, because he has seen it at work and has had much too close a view of it at that. His own good judgment requires him to back off. To back off several thousand kilometers.

Paris:

What Is a Pope?

Exactly what is a pope? A pope is sometimes called "the Vicar of Christ", an expression I have never been particularly fond of since the presence of a vicar suggests the absence of the Rector.

People also call the pope "the Sovereign Pontiff", but more and more rarely of late; and it's true he was once both pontiff and sovereign over several principalities that stretched across Italy like a strap across the top of a boot. Those days were all right for the people who lived in the Papal States but not so good for the Church, and government by the clergy got to be a convenient excuse for just the kind of anticlericalism that would later swing the pope's former subjects to the extreme political Left. It was an interesting trade-off, that the papacy had to divest itself of its territorial heritage for the sake of a united Italy and watch those lands shrink to the forty-four gilded hectares of Vatican City, while at the same time its power literally expanded right up into the skies—the more real estate the papacy lost, the more influential the office became. Not long ago, undoubtedly claiming this very precedent as justification, a group of Christians who purported to be desirous of extending the papacy's influence still further (and who thought it not robbery to call Pope Paul VI "Brother Paul") went so far as to suggest to him that he might do well to have Saint Peter's pulled down.[1] All the poor old basilica has ever done is to rise on winter mornings like a sun wrought in stone, and, just for that, for ages she has drawn a barrage of verbal brickbats aimed at her by iconoclasts; to them, beauty is a kind of sin they must avoid at all costs in order to safeguard their personal purity.

Considered solely in its religious sense, the term pontiff has a pagan connotation that is hard to get rid of: whenever I go on a trip to Rome, many times every day I pass by the obelisk in the Piazza Montecitorio, inscribed to the glory of Caesar Augustus, *pontifex maximus*. With such an undesirable philological past, the words *Sovereign Pontiff* risked being tainted with the tarbrush of implied idolatry, and this was a taint that alienated several generations of Catholics, especially in the old days when the ceremonial demanded that people multiply their genuflections before a being who seemed to have been hoisted above the ordinary human condition.

But that era of kowtowing and kindred abuses has declined since John XXIII, and besides, those were the days of anticlerical persecution. None of that business goes on any more under John Paul II. As if to anticipate what heaven will one day accomplish, the Catholic Faith simply exalts beyond measure whatever the secular world tries to bring low.

There are also some who would have the pope be merely "the Bishop of Rome"; of course, they would let him remain *primus inter pares*, "first among equals". But the precedence they would be willing to grant him would not include any notion of primacy. These men and women dream of a collegial form of church polity, something that inevitably brings to mind Trotsky's ferocious blast at the

[1] See Msgr. Jacques Martin, *Le Vatican inconnu* [Inside the Vatican] (Paris: Fayard, 1988).

members of the central committee who thought it would be a good idea to implement Lenin's policies according to their collective interpretations: "A College of Invalids can't take the place of the doctor!" To place the Church under the authority of a permanent assembly would be to defraud her of two of the three elements that constitute her unique and original character, for she is at once monarchical (the pope governs), aristocratic (the pope is chosen by the cardinals), and democratic (any man can be pope, no matter what his social class). This combination of Montesquieu's three Estates excited even Lenin's admiration. (I may perhaps be pardoned for mentioning these two eminent gurus of my ethnic subculture both in the same breath.) The partisans of democratization within the Church miss the mark the same way the liberals and conservatives do: they all fixate on the Church's structures, instead of turning to the One of whom the Church is only the reflection. The Church member who pays too much attention to the architecture of his parish church may well be running the risk of slighting the Blessed Sacrament.

The pope is also called "the successor of Peter", and this is an excellent definition of what a pope really is. Taken quite literally, it suggests that the pope is Peter's *immediate* successor, and not just a successor of all the popes in a long line. Thus, this definition makes it rather meaningless to compare one pope with another because each and every pope reigns in time to be a witness to those things that are eternal, and each and every one of them is the direct heir to Christ's own promise: "Thou art Peter, and upon this rock I will build my Church."

You may call my view naïve and I will cheerfully grant you that, but it certainly makes things a lot easier for me. For example, a pope is dressed in white, the color of fine flour.

They bring him out in front of crowds, who do not venerate him as a symbol of wheat, or even as the person that he is, but they respect his divinely ordained office, the institution of the papacy itself that is the source whence flow all the sacraments that nourish us, and the people bear witness to a presence that lies hidden, for a pope is a mystery, a pope is a kind of "Host". Sometimes, Hosts get broken.

Vézelay:

The Shepherd and the Gray Wolf

The basilica at Vézelay is a likeness of its holy patroness, the woman who had the most intuitive intelligence in the Gospels and who underwent the most striking conversion in history. The polychromed nave with its fine carvings resembles a richly brocaded oriental tunic, and the number of shadowy gargoyles that loom from the corner supports in the church seem to conjure up a medieval-nightmare version of psychoanalysis. The building as a whole, on the inside, gives a rather clear picture of Saint Mary Magdalen's life of temptation before her conversion, while the flying buttresses at one end of the nave that come down to meet the ground as graceful white columns portray the woman who was a sinner, coming to the Light; they are the wedding garment for the spiritual marriage of her who one day would announce to us Christ's Resurrection.

I was contemplating this riddle in stone when someone came and told me that an assassination attempt had just been made in Saint Peter's Square and that the Pope was dying. This crime had singled out, of all men on the face of this earth, the one man who was most peaceable. Once more Cain had raised his hand to smite Abel. In those first moments after I heard the news, it came back to me—my own first impression on his coronation day, when I saw him as a pope who looked just like one of the martyr-popes of apostolic times.

It was gloomy in the basilica and the gargoyles on the capitals grimaced more hideously than ever. Some days, symbols take on a life of their own, and I was at pains to find any consolation in the thought that these tiny imps imprisoned in stone and forced to support the vaulted ceiling could, in the long run, do anything to inspire good works in spite of themselves. Even the devil's henchman who had shot the Pope would, before long, raise enough arches of prayers and compassion to build a church within the Church herself; but while we waited, there was nothing we could do but cry.

Elsewhere[1] I have written about how, on May 13, 1981, during an outdoor audience, the Pope, attacked by a gunman who was caught and arrested as he fled, had been taken immediately to the ambulance that is always waiting by the colonnade around Saint Peter's Square on days when crowds will be coming in, and was then transferred to another ambulance that had better and more complete equipment (this ambulance had been offered to him the week before by the doctors of Rome, but its red light and siren had either not yet been connected or else were not in working order); and how the Pope's chauffeur, who is an expert at coping with traffic in Rome (an exact science and a school of hard knocks that grants precious few doctoral degrees), succeeded in getting to the Gemelli Hospital in eight minutes, a trip that normally takes experienced ambulance drivers half an hour; and how, as he was being rushed to the hospital, John Paul II said, more and more feebly as the moments passed, only Our Lady's name, Mary, and none of the things the newspapers attributed to him;

1 *"N'ayez pas peur!", dialogue avec Jean-Paul II* (Paris: Robert Laffont, 1982); English edition, *Be Not Afraid! John Paul II Speaks out on His Life, His Beliefs, and His Inspiring Vision for Humanity* (New York: Doubleday, 1984).

and how Professor Crucitti, a distinguished surgeon treating patients several kilometers away, narrowly made it to the hospital in time to operate on the victim, who was deathly pale from loss of blood but already stretched out on the operating table and draped in sterile sheeting. After the last sacraments had been administered to him, the Holy Father, his secretary kneeling at his side, the anesthesiologist straining to see his patient through eyes clouded with tears, and the surgical nursing nuns as the Holy Women, looked for all the world like a clinical icon of Jesus being taken down from the Cross, and, inasmuch as any priest, especially the Chief of Pastors, represents another Christ, no one found it at all odd that at that moment, somebody in the operating room murmured, "This is my Body, given for you." In conclusion I told how, after he had been under anesthesia for quite a long time, when he was just regaining consciousness, he asked his secretary, "Have we said compline?" You see how concerned he was lest the pistol shots of the day before keep him from finishing his Office, but that's the kind of sense of duty this Pope has, and he never relaxes it the least bit. His asking Don Stanislas that particular question while still in the recovery room ought to be included in any *fioretti* that get written up about his reign.

This attempted assassination had put his life at risk in two ways. First, he might have died from hemorrhage, and second, from an acute attack of a virus just as dangerous as Ali Agca's hail of gunfire. The killer's bullet had taken an unlikely path through the victim's body that missed all the vital organs, but it had pierced the intestine, and the Pope, when he arrived at the Gemelli Hospital, had already lost three and a half liters of blood; he rallied after he received extreme unction. A week later, he looked fine. But just when everyone thought his life had been saved, a new peril arose to

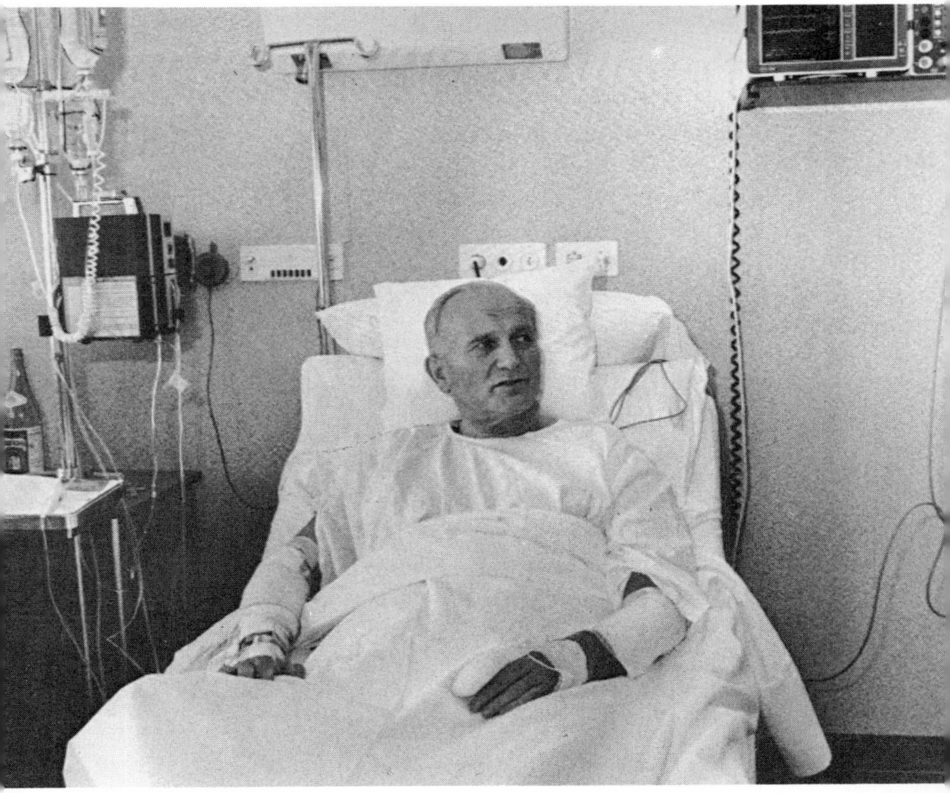

Pope John Paul II at the Gemelli Hospital, Rome.

threaten his survival. He had a rather rare blood type, so that the hospital's supply of blood for transfusions was exhausted. They had to issue an appeal for donors, and since urgency precluded extensive tests on the donated blood, one pint among all the pints collected in haste contained the infectious agent. The Pope came down with a very high fever that brutally jolted him back and forth from sweating as if it were midsummer to shivering as if he were in his shirtsleeves in the snows of Siberia. He was dying by inches every day. The doctors first thought he had picked up an infection as a complication of surgery and so they gave him antibiotics, but that did no good. Everyone was expecting the worst when researchers, who had been making test after test in the Biological Sciences Institute next door to the hospital, finally identified the contaminant that had caused all the trouble: it was a cytomegalovirus whose structure they most kindly showed me in a micrograph of the infinitesimal space between two cells, but such a picture only causes the uninitiated to marvel at the mystery of the abstract forms within an organism. The doctors replaced antibiotics with vitamins, and their patient's strong constitution did the rest. As a consequence of the assassination attempt Vatican Security provided him with the famous glassed-in "popemobile" that they now are in the habit of making him use to go about in crowds. Being hermetically sealed in the transparent, bulletproof vehicle exasperates him.

One day among guests he was receiving was a Polish lady whose marriage he had solemnized when he was in Cracow. He said as they sat at table, "All these precautions are useless. As soon as I go out, dressed in white from head to foot, I'm a target they can't possibly miss."

The lady was all for being prudent and took the side of the popemobile: "After all, the popemobile cuts down on the risk. We can't help being worried about Your Holiness."

Whereupon he, pretending to have taken this last expression literally, without capital letters, said evenly, "I'm worried about my holiness too."

The first state visit he received after the attempt on his life was that of the President of the Italian Republic, Sandro Pertini. The people of Italy were horrified that such a crime could have been committed within their borders, and there was nothing they feared more than the discovery of incontrovertible proof that the deed had been done by some common, ordinary terrorist gang that had eluded police for years. The Pope and the President quickly formed a cordial friendship, and Sandro Pertini's home is the only presidential residence John Paul II has ever honored with a personal visit. People saw the two of them walking together in the snow in the Dolomites, where the chief of state, who was having difficulty keeping his balance on a slippery slope, was holding onto the Pope's elbow for dear life: never before had the secular been so fervently joined to the spiritual arm. Another visitor of note, Mr. Fanfani, the well-known Christian Democrat member of parliament, came with a painting under his arm to see the Holy Father. It was one he had painted himself, depicting the Virgin Mary by means of intertwined, colored circles in the manner of the logo of the Olympic Games. The Pope admired it, thanked him profusely, and presented the work of art to his anesthesiologist, who was overcome with gratitude.

While he was hospitalized, the Pope never complained, never so much as groaned in all his pain, and never asked for anything. He was content with the two small rooms that had been placed at his disposal, he wore the same blue hospital gown all the other patients in the hospital wore, and during the two brief convalescences—the one following the initial surgery when he was getting over the virus and the one following the removal of the temporary colostomy apparatus that had given him such discomfort—he would walk up and down the corridor or visit the sisters' chapel on the same floor. When there was no room in the pews, he would kneel by the door. The nuns were amazed by his forbearance, and when they were asked what it was about their illustrious patient that had most impressed them, it took them no time at all to decide what to reply: it was his humility.

At the outset I too believed that the assassin must have been one of the terrorists who nowadays play the same destructive role in our society as the barbarians did in former times, terrorists who seem to have modeled their ideology on the hellish threat voiced by Stendhal's character who dreamed of "sweeping over the world like a cyclone, sowing the seeds of evil hither and yon on the wings of the wind". The man turned out to be a "Gray Wolf", a member of a little-known, right-wing extremist Turkish organization that committed murders wherever and whenever it pleased, for motives it alone could explain. Then we heard about the "Bulgarian Connection", and this information shifted Ali Agca's politics from the extreme Right to the extreme Left. The judges at his trial were unable to elicit any information from him: he must have received assurances that some kind of deal was in the works to get him off. Hit men who are caught in the act are more afraid of what their employers can do to them than they are of verdicts handed down by courts of law; only rarely do they consent to take the stand in their own defense. The Vatican sent no witnesses and pressed no charges, so the prosecution had no one on its bench to make the case for the State.

Some years later the Pope, who had already forgiven his would-be murderer a long time before then, went to visit Ali Agca in the Rebibbia Prison in Rome. The prisoner courteously invited him into his cell: "This is my home", he said with a touch of irony, but no more of his words could be heard, although the ever-present television set was abruptly turned off. Like a wolf, gray or not, Ali Agca has a sinuous way of moving and shifty eyes with a weird glint, which seems to turn his gaze to ice as soon as his prey comes within striking distance. He led his visitor to the back of the cell. Reporters and their cameramen were made to wait outside the door. The Pope sat down in an armchair, while Ali Agca sat in a straight chair. They talked for about half an hour, and neither of them moved more than a fraction of an inch the whole time. The Pope held onto Ali's arm, as if to pull him closer to him. Ali Agca bent over and whispered into the Holy Father's ear; no one could see Ali's face as he hid behind the profile of the Pope, who was perhaps at that moment hearing his confession. However, Turkish lip-reading specialists claimed to have been able to catch some of the words the Pope said. I told him about this, and he was curious to know what they thought he had said: "Holy Father, according to these men, the first thing you said was: 'Who wanted me dead?' "

He shrugged. So that couldn't have been right.

"What do they think I said next?"

"Next, they say you asked: 'Who sent you?' "

No shrug this time. So they were wrong on the first question but right on the second. The Pope neither confirmed nor denied it, and I could learn nothing more. There was only silence.

While the Holy Father was in the hospital, I did not dare go to Rome for fear of being a bother; perhaps it was also because of a long-standing timidity that I have never been able to overcome. Besides, I didn't think I had ever really *done* anything for him.

However, as soon as he was back at Castel Gandolfo, I

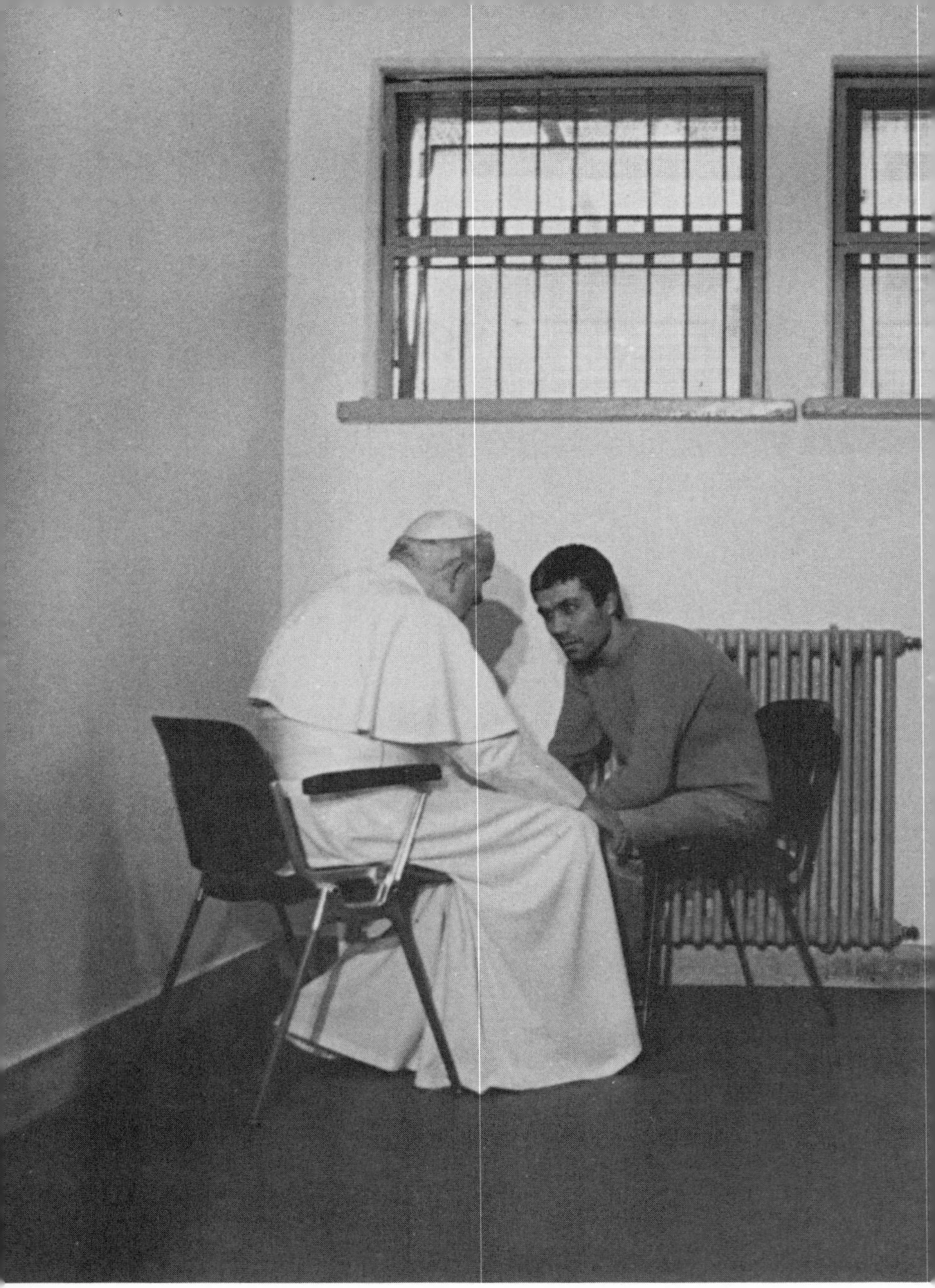

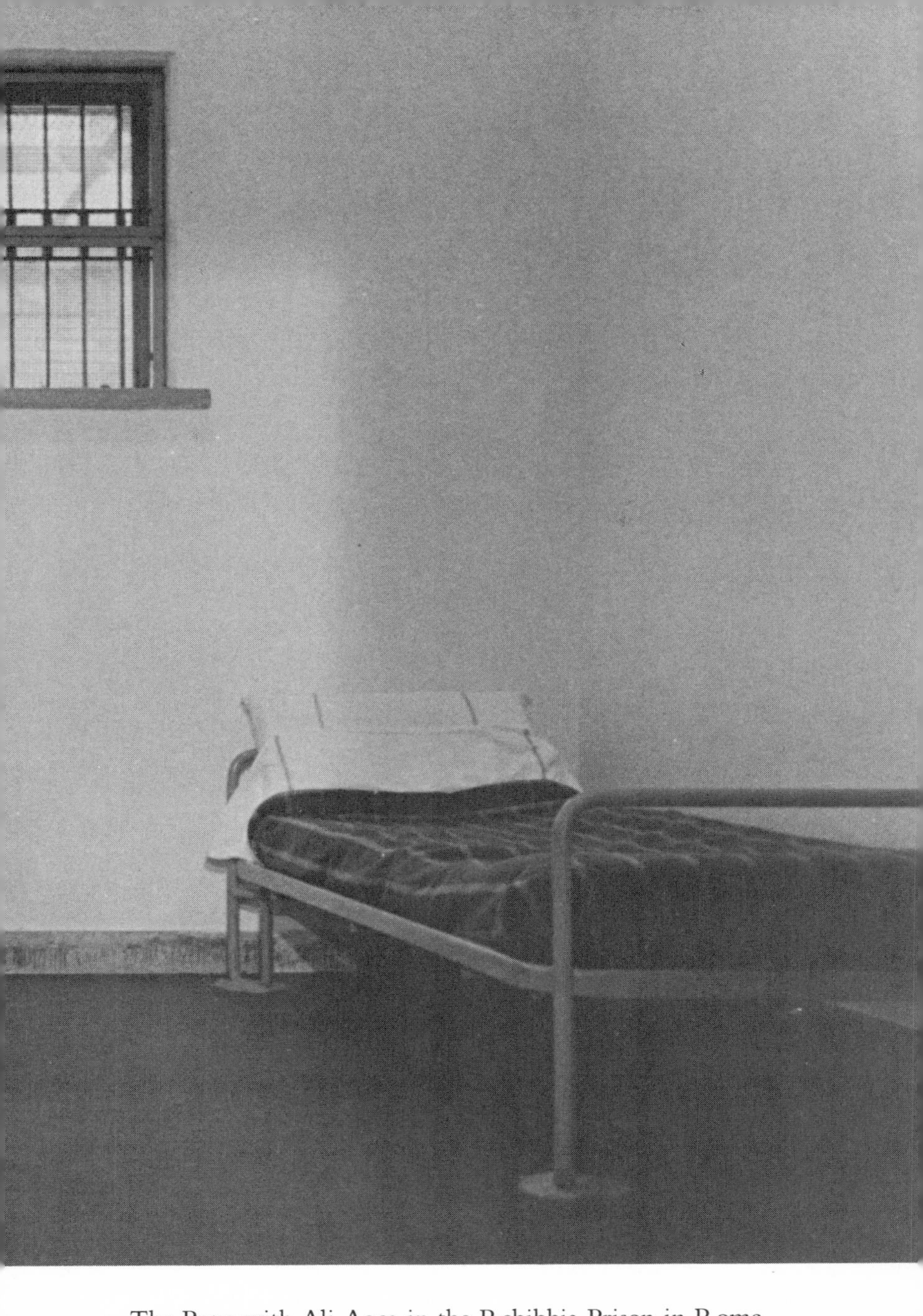

The Pope with Ali Agca in the Rebibbia Prison in Rome.

Pope John Paul II inside the "Popemobile".

hurried right over. My wife went with me. We found him with sunken cheeks, very thin, wearing what convalescent popes wear, that is, a white cassock without a mantelletta. I have never figured out how John Paul II, born and raised in a country whose climate in no way approximates that of the Bahamas, can stand to wear that white woolen cassock all through the summer in Rome when, as the locals say, "Only dogs and Frenchmen go out in the noonday sun". At any rate, we now saw clearly that we had had good reason to be afraid for his life, and we supposed he would need a long period of rest to make a full recovery. In fact, he took three weeks off, but he was by no means idle, even for that brief time.

At meals, he was given a tall glass of something that looked like fruit punch, vegetable-juice cocktail, or a tonic mixture of diverse ingredients that even my best efforts could not identify; he did not eat very much, for the doctors had put him on a rather Lenten diet. But, in one of their weaker moments, they had said he could have a glass of wine: he mentioned to us that this would be the first glass of wine he had had in a long time, and he wanted to drink it with us. Then he was surprised to see me sitting there with nothing in my hands. Hitherto, I had brought a few pages of our manuscript to the table with me, so that we could work on it between courses. "*I* did *my* work in the Gemelli", said he. So, since I had no typewritten text before me, I talked about how terrified all of us had been, and what a relief it had been to the whole world when we heard the news that the assassin's bullet had not touched any of his vital organs.

"That was a miracle," he said, "and I know whom I must thank for it. One hand was holding the gun, but Someone Else's hand was taking care of the bullet."

The assassination attempt had occurred on the anniversary of Our Lady's first apparition at Fatima, and he took that as a sign.

A sign that his work was not finished yet, and that there was nothing that could keep him from doing what he had to do. As for me, I thought the forces of evil had unleashed this murderous chain of events to no effect, proving that he had been doing what was right, and that, just as at Vézelay, the minions of the Office Down Below, jailed in stone, were again being compelled, by an army of angels the prayers of ordinary people had mustered, to bear up the Church's vault in spite of themselves.

Has this dreadful experience changed the Pope at all? He admits that sometimes he does not think he is "quite as efficient" as he was before, but that is not the opinion of his staff as they huff and puff trying to keep up with him just as they did in the good old days. Maybe he does tire a little more quickly than he used to; but then again, he is not so young now, and his custom of skimping on his evening meal, that leaves his stomach nearly empty until he has his breakfast coffee the next morning, is not exactly calculated to rejoice the body with marrow and fatness. Morally speaking, I have the impression that being so nearly mortally wounded not only served as a testimony to his faith, but also must surely have anchored him more deeply in his practice of abandonment of his whole self to God's Divine Will, a principle that guides his entire spiritual life. The martyr-popes of the early Church were no braver than he is. This latest in their line has passed through the fire and come out alive.

Rome:

Suffering and Love

From his youth, the Pope has known what it is to suffer: he was left all alone in life while he was still no more than a child. No one knows how much pain he had to go through as a result of the attempt on his life of May 13, 1981; he never complained then, and never in his life has he been one to complain. The little nuns who cared for him in the hospital admired what the secular world would probably call his "stoicism", something that for him is a different thing altogether. He is fully aware of what it takes to participate in the redemptive suffering of his Lord, that suffering Saint Paul referred to when he said, "Now I rejoice in my sufferings for your sake, and in my flesh I complete what is lacking in Christ's afflictions for the sake of his body, that is, the Church . . ." (Col 1:24). He is light-years ahead of today's bleeding hearts who talk of the dehumanizing effect of suffering, since pain diminishes him not at all, but rather spurs him on to greater things.

To his mind, there is but one final degradation: to lose eternal life. He writes in his apostolic letter "On the Christian Meaning of Human Suffering" (*Salvifici doloris*) "The Son of God was given to us to save us from this ultimate evil. . . . Human suffering has reached its culmination in the Passion of Christ. At the same time, it has entered into a completely new dimension and a new order: it has been linked to love" (no. 18).

This miraculous joining of suffering with love is familiar to the mystics. How would we ever be sure we had been in love, had truly loved someone, if we did not feel the anguish of separation, and what would connect us with the otherworldly reality of love if not this diamond, that serves as proof that we have loved enough to endure suffering for love's sake?

I wonder what those people who consider suffering demeaning make of the Cross of Christ.

The Holy Father told me, "When I was young, sick people used to intimidate me." He shied away from looking straight at people who were obviously in agonizing pain. They bore in their bodies a dread mystery, whose entire meaning would later be revealed to him: people who are ill bring charity into being, "the weak are a source of strength" (see 2 Corinthians 12:9). He said to someone I know, the night before that friend was to undergo a major operation: "I am entrusting the Church to you."

People used to talk about the "sacrament of the sick". I think that in his own way of looking at things, the Holy Father considers every sick person to be ipso facto a kind of sacrament.

Castel Gandolfo:

Humility

Humility is certainly one of John Paul II's most deeply rooted character traits.

It is his humility that makes him so openhearted, so kindly disposed precisely toward the humble and toward children. Whenever he enters the large audience chamber at the Vatican, he stops to greet the people in the top rows all the way in the back, the ones in the least desirable places farthest from the throne. He listens to them, responds to them, shakes as many hands as possible. The time he spends at each level diminishes proportionally as he gets closer to the front row reserved for persons of rank, the ones who are not always lucky enough to get to speak a word to him. He has to stand apart as Pope, as head of the Church, only when he is among chiefs of state and highly placed individuals who cross his path for political reasons or to satisfy their own curiosity. With ordinary people, he is a brother among his brethren, the brother responsible for rooting and grounding them all in the Faith. Even though he has been made the successor of Peter, under no circumstances would he promenade around jangling the keys of the kingdom; on the contrary, the tremendous responsibility gives him a feeling that is anything but one of superiority.

This humility of his naturally brings him close to children, who typify what those who want to enter the kingdom of heaven must be like. The most touching among all the countless such moments in his reign has to be that unforgettable time the Pope embraced a little boy afflicted with AIDS, hugging the child and holding him exactly the way the priest, at the end of Benediction, carries the Blessed Sacrament close to his heart.

It is, moreover, the practice of this basic virtue that is not much in vogue in our generation, that leads him to back up the statements he makes with multiple citations from the Gospels, from Saint Paul, and from the Second Vatican Council. We find these references throughout his writings. When we were working together on our book *"Be Not Afraid!"*, I had to read all the constitutions and declarations of Vatican II from cover to cover, and often several times, in order to make sure I was following the reasoning behind what he said in his answers to my questions, and I must confess that until then I had not been very conversant with the documents the Council formulated. But this required reading incidentally made it possible for me to prove that John Paul II has been very faithful to the Council's thrust and that its views were not so revolutionary as the rightists (who wanted something to complain about) and the leftists (who were looking for something to gloat over) attempted to make us believe.

He places no more than a modest reliance on his own intellect, a mind that is, needless to say, uncommonly keen. Whenever he has to work out a doctrinal matter, he conforms his explanations to the teachings of the Church Fathers, and at every stage he makes certain his words are consistent with what is laid down in Holy Scripture, so that he can use both these sources as pitons. He never attempts a "first ascent" up the "North Face" of any dogma without previously consulting his well-tried Sherpas, the expert theologians in the Church: there still are some, even in Rome.

It is from this very same humility, manifesting itself in his gentleness and in his genius that is truly an infinite capacity for taking pains, that he derives the stamina to keep on until he finishes a lengthy exposition. Staying with the mountain-climbing analogy, he could, if he preferred, take the quick way straight up the vertical granite escarpment, the route Italian alpinists call the *direttissima* (most direct), but besides being careful not to lead other people onto a path where they might stumble, he is concerned lest taking shortcuts cause him to neglect a point of view that might be helpful to his neighbor. This is why his presentations are so often reminiscent of mountain trails that sometimes must descend in order to reach the safest place to begin climbing again, or of ledges where the mountaintop looks farther away than ever when actually the climber is almost there.

It is a problem these days to find anyone willing to listen to an exhortation on this miraculous virtue, so disparaged by the upwardly mobile who talk only of "self-realization" and "self-expression", and who preface everything they say with the words, "As for *me personally*, I . . ." Yet it is humility, mere humility, that casts the key great thinkers turn to unlock the mysteries of the universe. The scientist who did not feel finite beholding the minuscule particles and organisms in nature would never make a breakthrough; the philosopher who did not stand in awe before the object of all his reasoning would end by contemplating nothing but his own navel, and we are all familiar with what a modern painter who has no humility can do to the beautiful forms God has created: that's what's called modern art.

As one who is genuinely humble, John Paul II judges no one. He puts up with anyone at all judging him. But he wrinkles his nose at the smell of the incense when the thurible swings in his direction.

The day I took him the first chapter of our dialogue to read at the table, its very first sentence nearly spoiled his appetite.

I had written, "By taking the name John Paul II, he was discreetly allowing his predecessors to put him in the shade, but you cannot shut out the light of the sun." He raised his eyes from the manuscript and turned toward me with a disappointed look.

"You're sure that's a proper comparison? Can't you find any other way?"

I liked it the way I had it, so I undertook to defend my opening phrases by saying that there is nothing more important than the first sentence of a book, and that what I'd written expressed my thoughts to the letter. He did not insist. But the next day, he brought up the subject again: "All the same, the sun . . ."

I saw I was upsetting him. I scratched it out, to his great relief.

Need I say it? I certainly had no intention of using this bit of text (that so nearly got us into an argument) to flatter him; I was just venting an enthusiasm that up to now had had very few outlets.

Rome:

A Major Spiritual Lesson

The Pope prays with every breath he takes.

In the morning, he starts his prayers well before Mass, and he follows his Mass with a more or less lengthy time of thanksgiving. During the day, he frequently pauses in the midst of work or conversation and goes into a "meditation-block"; staff members are accustomed to this practice and understand that they simply have to wait it out in silence. In the midst of liturgical ceremonies, when the rubrics call for one genuflection, he sometimes makes three or four or else kneels down and stays down for several minutes: young masters of ceremonies who would not dare tug at his sleeve have no idea how to bring him back to earth and so they just allow the ritual to hang there in a state of suspended animation. One of the most burdensome of all his duties undoubtedly is having to listen to disquisitions their authors seem to think need to be spun out for as long as possible before coming to the point. He listens, obviously with the kindest possible attention, but if you are seated close enough to him you will be able to spot the beads of his rosary moving quietly between his fingers. What do you imagine he is praying about at times like those?

"Holy Father, how do you pray?"

That is an intrusive question. He is so polite that he found it only a delicate one, and he answered it in his own way, a way that most often is wholly unpredictable: "Adrienne von Speyr writes about how well-known men of the past prayed. For example, Shakespeare, Dante. She had revelations. I'm just reading her now."

Adrienne von Speyr was a Swiss woman, a convert from Protestantism to Catholicism. In her childhood, she had seen visions, and the great theologian Hans Urs von Balthasar helped her found the Society of Saint John the Evangelist. She died several years after founding the Society.

"She says that in spite of the reputation for energy he acquired as a result of his condemnations of Nazism and communism, Pius XI was really a timid man. I wonder what she would say about the way I pray. It's a very personal subject."

So personal that all the time I was asking my question, I was telling myself I would have done better to keep my mouth shut, and that is why, after asking, "Holy Father, how do you pray?" I added immediately, "or, if that is too much to ask, how would you advise us to pray?"

"I'm going to tell you a story. When I was ten or twelve years old, I was a choirboy, but I wasn't very dedicated, I must confess. My mother wasn't with us any more. . . . But my father, when he found out how sloppy my discipline was, said to me one day, 'You are not being a very good choirboy. You don't pray to the Holy Spirit enough. You ought to pray to him.' And he taught me a prayer to say."

"And you haven't forgotten it?"

"I certainly haven't. That was a major spiritual lesson, longer-lasting and more powerful than anything I got from my reading or from the courses I took later on. What conviction his voice held as he told me that! I can still hear his voice saying those words, even today. The end-product of that lesson from my childhood is my encyclical on the Holy Spirit."

Only by the remotest chance would any of the little discussions of religion we have, usually by accident, with our children, ever produce an encyclical. However, we cannot predict what fruits our words will bear. Just when we think they are gone forever, one fine day we discover they have grown like the mustard seed in the parable (see Mt 13:31), to be great trees.

> In my youth, I would pray to obtain whatever gifts of the Holy Spirit seemed most intriguing at the time. Then I found out what Saint Paul meant when he gave us the last word on the subject in his Epistle to the Romans: "Likewise the Spirit helps us in our weakness; for we do not know how to pray as we ought, but the Spirit himself intercedes for us with sighs too deep for words" (Rom 8:26). I do not see any other way to explain my personal way of praying except by this verse from Saint Paul. In the last analysis, it is always the Holy Spirit who interprets our prayers—*and he is greater than we are.*

The Holy Father went on to say: "God took a terrible risk when he created us—he gave us our freedom. But he helps that freedom to find its completeness in love. All the gifts of the Holy Spirit imply love, starting with the 'fear of God' that is the beginning of wisdom."

What the Holy Father sees as the "fear of God" does not consist in quaking beneath his almighty and terrible hand like characters in some seventeenth-century tragedy. It is more like the wonder that makes us hold babies as if they might break.

Rome:

John Paul II's Philosophy

His thought has been studied from every angle, and there are plenty of angles in it to study. As far as I can see, it takes the form of a cathedral whose architecture is a composite of many styles, a cathedral built over the mighty vault of a Roman crypt whose pillars are the principles of the philosophy of being, that kind of philosophy that "comes naturally to the human mind", as Bergson put it. The entrance to the great church is the door of faith, its nave of hope leads to the holy sacrament of divine charity; the dome over the transept rests on four columns, the cardinal virtues (prudence, justice, temperance, fortitude), and the seven gifts of the Holy Spirit (Is 11:2ff.) surround the choir, framing it with arches that evoke both intertwining branches and spreading wings. To the left of the altar stands the angel of the Annunciation, and at the right the Virgin Mary, who first spoke Jesus' name with human voice. The stained glass windows shine forth the whole spectrum of human consciousness in all its miraculous colors. The entire edifice stands as a classical unity of prayer, adoration and the patient seeking of the Will of God. Its architect's methodology is ordered like a liturgy that begins with the creation of the world and continues straight through to the ultimate fulfillment of the promises of the gospel. The most meaningful reading in its Divine Office is perhaps this passage from Saint Luke:

> So they watched him, and sent spies, who pretended to be sincere, that they might take hold of what he said, so as to deliver him up to the authority and jurisdiction of the governor. They asked him, "Teacher, we know that you speak and teach rightly, and show no partiality, but truly teach the way of God. Is it lawful for us to give tribute to Caesar, or not?"

(If he answered "Yes", he would grant his approval to his people's subjection to the Roman yoke; if he said "No", he would be inciting rebellion against Roman authority.)

> But he perceived their craftiness, and said to them, "Show me a coin. Whose likeness and inscription has it?" They said, "Caesar's." He said to them, "Then render to Caesar the things that are Caesar's, and to God the things that are God's" (Lk 20:19–25).

According to Scripture, the human being was created in God's image: if what bears Caesar's stamp is to be given to Caesar, then man, made in God's image, belongs to God. It is in God alone, and not in himself, that man will find his identity. This, it seems to me, must be the root of the personalism that makes the Holy Father's moral theology unique.

Newman used to say, "I and my Creator". I have the impression that for John Paul II, that "I" is superfluous. Man is a copy in search of his original.

Castel Gandolfo:

Original Sin

The Pope is talking about original sin, and he quotes me the old serpent's deceitful suggestion:

> The serpent . . . said to the woman . . . "You may eat . . . of the fruit of the tree which is in the midst of the garden, 'the tree of the knowledge of good and evil', and you will not die. For God knows that when you eat of it your eyes will be opened, and you will be like God, knowing good and evil" (see Gen 3:1–5).

For the Pope, as it was for Saint Augustine, the first of all sins and the root of every sin afterward was "that love of self that makes a man turn his back on God". I think I understand that the fall of Adam was a fall the creature brought on himself, when he chose himself rather than his creator, and it was not merely an isolated happening at the dawn of history, but a temptation that replicates itself from generation to generation. Even if it does not always cause a man to "forsake God utterly", that is what it tends toward. The first man was "swayed by the Tempter's assurance that eating of the fruit of that tree would help him to acquire knowledge". The Pope picks up an apple from a basket that has just been brought to the table, looks at it for a moment and says thoughtfully: "It really is a beautiful thing, this piece of fruit. But was it necessary to sacrifice everything for it? It's all anybody cares about any more."

He draws an infinite number of conclusions from this story in Genesis that he calls "extraordinarily profound", that effectively contains just about everything it might be important to know about the human condition. And, while he is talking, I have a flashback of the feeling I had the day I got my first close view of the newly cleaned frescoes in the Sistine Chapel: when I watched that sort of black tide, rolling back under the skillful hands of the restorers as they carefully sponged off soot and grime, receding from the vaults it had so long obscured and bringing the people Michelangelo had painted back to the light they were made of in the first place. Going up and down the aisles from bay to bay was like looking at Michelangelo's work before and after a cataract operation. It has the same effect on people when John Paul II explains Genesis: with all the accumulation of mud from century after century of fashionably bored disbelief washed off, the Garden of Eden reappears in its original colors.

Castel Gandolfo:

The Value of Human Life

Not being a physician or a priest, I generally try to stay off subjects like this one. But it has to be faced, since the average Christian seems to be unwilling to talk about anything else.

John Paul II's teaching on contraception and abortion has been opposed with a vigor directly proportional to people's abysmal misunderstanding of it. It has been so badly misunderstood that some won't even listen to it any more. The only fault one could legitimately find with it, a fault that really ought to make us all feel a lot better, might be that it reads like it places too high a value on the human person.

Nobody on earth that has the sense he was born with could imagine a pope who would permit abortion. Abortion is murder.

> In the Middle Ages [the Pope says], it was thought that the developing being passed through a vegetable phase, then into an animate phase, and so forth; thus the responsibility for interrupting a pregnancy might not have seemed so serious to tender consciences: some might have believed that they were only putting an end to a plant or to an animal. Today, that sort of rationalizing is no longer possible. The human being exists from the moment of conception. Modern medicine uses other ways to express that, but as for us, we say that even as an embryo, a baby is already marked with the image of God.

I happened to have a brief chance to observe a baby in the very early stages of prenatal development, in an image projected onto a monitor by a sonograph. And didn't it look, in perspective, as if this very tiny beginning of a baby were coming from a far country beyond the horizon, or even right from heaven? It was as if the baby, waving his little arms as best he could, were shouting: "Wait for me, wait for me! I'm coming!"

Looking at it from the baby's point of view, we are talking about a person here.

> And if the person, [the Pope continues] is what is most important, then one cannot say anything but what I have just said, and there are no two ways about it. Because here it is a question of what we are, and of what we will become. Even before *Humanae vitae* I was already certain that we were dealing with something that mankind cannot do away with if he is to have a future.

Pontifical documents most often treat questions relating to contraception and abortion together, even though the two matters may appear quite separate at first glance.

> People say let's stamp out abortion, but allow the use of artificial contraceptives. But to permit the use of artificial contraceptives is the same as to open the way for abortion, because the moral attitude is what counts in this instance. Human life is an absolute value, tied up with the creative power of God. It is not "manipulable".

He never separates man from God. From this it follows that there exists an intangible truth in human relationships, in human love. And he has a saying, one of the most beautiful things I've ever heard him say: "There is no love without truth."

He goes on to say: "The distinction you want so much to

make between artificial contraception and abortion has always been made. If two things do not have the same stigma attached to them, then one does not seem to be quite so serious as the other."

Nobody is judging anybody else. As for the acts themselves, they cannot be judged independently of the circumstances that brought about their commission. Even in the case of an abortion, that abortion has to be judged "in the same way as every other attempt on human life would be judged".

Does this mean that a husband and wife cannot make love except for purposes of procreation?

> God knows us intimately. He has placed limits on the numbers of opportunities women may have to conceive children. Birth control by natural methods is licit. All these artificial means of birth control, no matter which ones we might enumerate, are the reason why Western civilization is in the mess it is in today.

In the Holy Father's way of thinking, God is not the kind of creator who would abandon his work, leaving us to fend for ourselves by our own logic. God is not a judge who sits waiting for the hour of our death or for the end of time, to weigh mankind in the balance and try us by the sword of his inexorable justice. God is not a being enthroned in some unknown place beyond the universe: he is the God who exists in the here and now. He is somehow implied in the very fact of our human personality and so also in our procreation. Morality should be determined by our more or less clear realization that we do have this presence of God within us.

Rome:

Sin and the Sitz im Leben

What is the gravest danger mankind is exposed to nowadays? Whenever I asked the Holy Father that question, he answered: "Sin."

And because his way of thinking never leaves its home territory in the landscape of revelation except with a sigh of regret, he called to my attention how "the Lord saw that the wickedness of man was great in the earth" (Gen 6:5) before the flood, and he reminded me of how exasperated God was with his creature. He noted that an echo could be found in the first chapter of Saint Paul's Epistle to the Romans: "But the Cross has redeemed all things. God does not reject this world" (see Rom 5:8–10).

My curiosity prompted me to reread this chapter from Saint Paul, a passage I never considered to have anything to do with the sixth chapter of Genesis. Nobody quotes much from the first chapter of Romans now. It's too bad they don't. When I looked it up, I found that in Romans it is a question of another kind of flood, the kind of flood where the human conscience can die by drowning in sin:

> For the wrath of God is revealed from heaven against all ungodliness and wickedness of men who by their wickedness suppress the truth. For what can be known about God is plain to them, because God has shown it to them. Ever since the creation of the world his invisible nature, namely, his eternal

> power and deity, has been clearly perceived in the things that have been made. So they are without excuse; for although they knew God they did not honor him as God or give thanks to him, but they became futile in their thinking and their senseless minds were darkened. Claiming to be wise, they became fools. . . .
>
> Therefore God gave them up in the lusts of their hearts to impurity, to the dishonoring of their bodies among themselves, because they exchanged the truth about God for a lie and worshiped and served the creature rather than the Creator, who is blessed for ever! Amen.
>
> For this reason God gave them up to dishonorable passions. Their women exchanged natural relations for unnatural, and the men likewise gave up natural relations with women and were consumed with passion for one another, men committing shameless acts with men and receiving in their own persons the due penalty for their error (Rom 1:18–22; 24–26).

If that doesn't strike you as being so bad, just hang on. There's more:

> And since they did not see fit to acknowledge God, God gave them up to a base mind and to improper conduct. They were filled with all manner of wickedness, evil, covetousness, malice. Full of envy, murder, strife, deceit, malignity, they are gossips, slanderers, haters of God, insolent, haughty, boastful, inventors of evil, disobedient to parents, foolish, faithless, heartless, ruthless. Though they know God's decree that those who do such things deserve to die, they not only do them but approve those who practice them (Rom 1:28–32).

When he wrote that, of course, Saint Paul was thinking about the pagans. He must have been. It must just be a lack of appreciation for modern textual criticism that made one think one was reading the morning newspaper.

Rome:

Total Defense of Humanity

If the big event of the Pope's reign was the assassination attempt that could easily have put an end to his pontificate, but, thank goodness, fell short of its goal, his reign's grand design was the defense of humanity. It was total defense, just as we once spoke of total war, and it mobilized and went into action either successively or simultaneously on the political front, the social front, the moral front, and the spiritual front.

I could mention one French philosopher whose errors dazzled everybody in the coffeehouses around Saint-Germain-des-Prés for many years, a man who claimed there was no such thing as human nature, an assertion that more than one ape must have found entirely satisfactory. As Aristotle quipped, "There is no absurdity in the world that cannot find at least one philosopher to defend it."

With or without a nature, however, man is threatened today as he has never been before. When Aldous Huxley published *Brave New World* in 1932, he conservatively predicted that bottled babies and happiness pills would be available to us within six hundred years. In the preface to the 1941 edition, he shortened the wait, bringing it down to one hundred years. Hardly half that century has run its course and here we are: we already have our test-tube babies (I'll get back to them in a minute), our mothers and even our surrogate grandmothers capable of bearing children by their sons-in-law, grandmothers whose grandsons, who are also their sons, are in addition their legal mothers' brothers; experiments in crossing one species with another, excising a baboon's heart and transplanting it into a human baby (who died, of course); plotting elaborate series of experiments in such attention-getting concepts as animal-to-human organ transplants, so that a live-organ donor might some day be a pig that would not think itself too terribly déclassé if it were asked to part with a heart or a trotter; stockpiling frozen embryos; euthanasia administered arbitrarily (in *Brave New World* youth extends to age sixty, and then meets its swift and painless end); and genetic engineering, still on a very primitive level at present but I doubt they'll take long to try out on man the techniques they have found so successful in veal production, if I understand aright the considered opinions of certain meat packers.

All this follows from the commonplace idea that man is just another animal like all the rest; but that idea is a false one: animals are finished products, man is not. What sense would there be in putting more fur on a cat? Admirably formed, pleasingly lithe, he is totally, absolutely, and serenely cat. Man is incomplete, and he knows it. He is never absolutely and serenely man. He is a cat who will never be satisfied until he learns how to bark. His consciousness of his own imperfection is his window into infinity, a window that also lets him in for all the temptations attendant upon that vision, the most serious being the temptation to lower himself to that perfected state that belongs to his "lesser brothers", who ask no questions of themselves or of anyone else.

And I haven't even mentioned mind control, psychological experiments more to be feared than the biological ones noted above, and all the more to be dreaded for the very reason that they are as yet not perceived to be at all hazardous to health. Elegant studies have been put together on the effects of "subliminal imaging" introduced into a film to sell an industrial product or to create support for some political aim, and these subliminal images imprint themselves on the brain before the eye has even had time to focus on them; but because they flash on and off the screen so fast, all pictures on television today tend to function as subliminal images. Their message is simple: the world is in a continual state of flux, movement, and change without beginning and without end, and contemplation is impossible.

The Pope fights with all his strength to keep the Brave New World from coming into existence. He would find it a lonely campaign but for those few concerned scientists who worry about how the power we learn to exercise over living matter today might be wielded tomorrow. The Holy Father published his own carefully documented, minutely detailed instruction on *in vitro* fertilization and other related techniques, only to see it rejected out of hand not just by those idolaters of progress determined to prove Jean-Paul Sartre right in his boast that "no such thing as human nature exists", but even by researchers in a Catholic medical school who decided to keep on with their experiments in the sincere belief that their present inability to evaluate their results must mean something big was just around the corner.

Is there anyone living who is completely insensitive to the plight of married couples who have wanted a baby of their own for years only to have nature seem to deny their wish? Who could be unsympathetic toward husbands and wives who are prepared to go through anything, even the emotional pressure, discomfort, and inconvenience of fertility tests and treatments, in the hope of having their own child? All the same, though, how can we ignore the fact that between the test tube and implantation, the embryo may be subjected to the most extraordinary, even the most absurd manipulations, and the fertilized ovum placed in the same petri dish with ten or twenty others to be frozen or destroyed, its chances of survival being about the same as those of surviving an airplane crash? A laboratory crèche is not without its wasteproducts, and sometimes there are street-sweepers instead of shepherds around the crib.

Every one of John Paul II's encyclicals has to do with some aspect of human life or human activity, and in the same way, all his addresses—unless they are pure mystical poetry such as his exquisite prayer to Our Lady of Lourdes—plead for social justice and sincere goodwill among men.

Certainly, he would have us understand that all the popes have always spoken for the good of souls, for the welfare of mankind, for the preservation of the integrity of the image of God that man bears within himself, even when he sees only its blurred reflection in the distorting mirrors that changing styles and ideologies hold before his face. If we are the least bit fair, we will concentrate not on what popes have said that was out of keeping with the spirit of their times (anyhow, popes are not there to be servants of the *Zeitgeist*), but rather we will recognize that they have always taken, as far as public and private morals are concerned, the noblest position, the stance that is not necessarily the most popular. In any case, John Paul II never misses an opportunity to pay tribute to their work and to make reference to their writings.

Nonetheless, his untiring pilgrimage throughout the world and his powerful personality combine to make him the first pope in history who can be called not "postconciliar" but "postrevolutionary", since the vast majority of the peoples of the world recognize in him the surest and most faithful defender of human rights. If you had announced such a finding fifty or even thirty years ago, people would have said you were skewing your data.

Lourdes:

John Paul II's Prayer to Our Lady

I just said something about John Paul II's prayer to Our Lady of Lourdes. Here are a few lines from it. In these lines, you are going to hear his heart speaking:

> O Woman clothed with the Sun . . .[1]
>
> You wear the Sun of Christ like a mantle, the Sun of the redemption of the world and of mankind by the Cross and Resurrection of your Son; and you have sheltered all of us poor sons of Eve under this protecting mantle, while we live here on earth in this our exile.
>
> Let that Sun shine unceasingly on us on earth!
>
> Do not permit that Sun to be darkened in men's souls.
>
> Let it illumine the way for the Church on the road of her earthly pilgrimage, for you are her pattern and archetype.
>
> O Mother of our Redeemer, help the Church always to keep her eyes fixed on you, so that she may continually increase and grow as our Mother here on earth by learning Motherhood from you!
>
> O Mother, defend the sons and daughters of earth from the death of the soul!
>
> Be a witness for God for all mankind, because man's eyes are blinded by his passion to rule the world, and he may become so captivated by worldly things that he may lose even the vision of his eternal home in God. Be a witness for God for all mankind; be a witness for God!

[1] See Rev 12:1.

Rome:

Sayings of the Holy Father

He says: "Liberty is the measure of how much love we are capable of giving."

He says further: "The Church is a sacrament, a visible sign. And so is man. He is the 'visibility of the invisible'."

What leads him to use such a striking, unusual image is this: "For the Latin *Abyssus*—there is no better definition. Man is a spiritual abyss."

When labeled a "conservative": "I am not offended. The pope is not here to make changes, but to conserve what he has received into his charge [see 1 Tim 6:20]. In Saint John, Christ says: 'I [say] nothing on my own authority but speak thus as the Father taught me' [see Jn 8:28]. This commandment holds for all the apostles as well; I am profoundly convinced of it."

What must we fear nowadays?

"Everything that does not come from God, and that purports to represent progress."

On the worst evil of our time: "It is not so much the overt denial of God as it is the temptation to live as if he did not exist."

I asked him which verse from the Gospel he would choose if he could bequeath us only one to live by. I thought he would take some time to pick one out. I was mistaken. He answered without a moment's hesitation: "The truth shall make you free" (Jn 8:32).

Rome:

The Strait Gate and Narrow Way of Ecumenism

People reproach the Pope for not possessing sufficient ecumenical spirit as often as they accuse him of being too ecumenically minded.

Some would prefer him to sacrifice doctrine for the sake of unity, but others cannot forgive him for gathering around himself at Assisi representatives of all, or almost all, the religions of the world.

As far as the first group is concerned, it would satisfy them if the Catholic Church relaxed her doctrinal standards enough to let in all who call themselves Christians; they imagine that such a surrender would induce all Christians to throw themselves into each other's arms. Since faith in Jesus Christ as Messiah and Savior is common to every denomination, why not just pile everybody's sandbags on this broad dike of faith so as to stem the flood of materialism, atheism, and apathy that has already inundated three-fourths of the globe, and even now threatens to engulf the remainder?

As for the second group, the Catholic Church is the only legitimate repository of truth, and this gives her certain rights over people's consciences that she cannot relinquish without forfeiting her claim to being the One True Church. Whoever does not recognize her preeminence and universal Magisterium is a heretic and a schismatic; ecumenism is a temptation of the Evil One, something it is every Catholic's duty to resist.

Between these two positions lies a narrow road that twists and turns and often doubles back upon itself. For a long time I asked myself why Catholics and Protestants, while able to maintain cordial and amicable relationships on a personal basis, had so much trouble understanding each other when it came to religion, even on points where they didn't seem to disagree; then I remembered my country village, Montbéliard and thereabouts, where the population was made up of pietists (Reformed) and a few isolated Lutherans like my maternal grandparents. The pietists worshipped without the aid of either pastors or sacraments, relying on texts from the Bible alone, principally from the Old Testament, and often named their children Ruth or Abraham. In its zeal to get back to the source, their denomination had crossed the bar of the New Testament and was scudding along on course toward the beginning of time. Always prepared to quote you chapter and verse, they were something like the American pioneers who went West with their Bibles under their arms, ever ready, as it occurred to me to write, "to whip out the Bible and reel off verses to stop a hero about to do something really brave dead in his tracks, or to select at random from the Book some out-of-context quotation predicting an outcome that had nothing to do with the situation". They looked askance at the Lutherans, whom they regarded as backsliders, while the Lutherans got even by reproaching them for giving the impression that they were only half-Reformed. However great their differences may have been, they partook of the same scornful attitude toward the Catholics. Was that attitude something that harked back to the wars of religion, those centuries of hatred and persecution? Undoubtedly. Were there insurmountable doctrinal differences separating them? Maybe, although Lutheran and Catholic terminology, when it came to talking about faith, did not seem divergent enough to warrant such hostility. There had to be something more.

When my conversion made it possible for me to get to know Catholics as well as I knew the Protestants in my childhood, I noticed a fact that would seem obvious to most people, although it was not such a commonplace for me. It was that a Protestant was a Christian who had no doubts, for the very sensible reason that his whole religion rested upon his private conscience in such a way that he could hardly doubt God without doubting himself. A Catholic, on the other hand, being required to believe dogmata that stretched his reasoning faculty beyond comfortable limits, doubted often, doubted much, and when he could not resolve his doubts relied on the counsel of his parish priest, his bishop, or the pope to help his unbelief. These two radically different psychologies that could not help failing to come to agreement nevertheless did not stand in the way of personal friendships at all, but they made it difficult for the denominations to find common ground, and, even if they could have found it in their hearts to leave off consigning one another to hell all the time, they were still a long way from full communion. After years of zealous ecumenical activity, the project of nominating a new Bishop of Geneva (where the Catholics now slightly outnumber the Calvinists) so polarized the town that they had to attach the diocese to another canton to keep the factions from running amok and spoiling everything they had accomplished.

Now for the Anglicans and the Orthodox. Anglicans are not all alike. Some of them lean toward Protestantism, others lean so far toward Catholicism that they sometimes give the impression that all they are waiting for, before they

Pope John Paul II addresses the multitude in St. Peter's Square.

reunite with Rome, is the completion of the tunnel under the English Channel. The difference between the Orthodox and the Catholics seems to be little other than the length of matins and vespers; their doctrines are like twin sisters you can tell apart only by the color of their dresses. The ordinary church member finds the disputes that broke the Church's unity almost a thousand years ago well-nigh incomprehensible. He has heard tell that the Western clergy want the Holy Spirit to proceed "from the Father and the Son", while the Eastern clergy want him to proceed only "from the Father"; to the average person, that doesn't seem to constitute grounds for divorce, and he can't help thinking that if this unfortunate argument proves anything, it proves that the Holy Spirit had nothing to do with it.

Outside of that, the Creed is the same: "Doctrinally," the Pope told me, "the Orthodox are very close to us, but psychologically they are very far away. It's the opposite with the Anglicans. There exist serious doctrinal differences between them and us, but nowadays we never cease trying to get together."

I don't know if he would say the same thing now that the Anglican Bishops in England, under pressure, it would seem, from Anglicans in America, lean toward admitting women to the priesthood.

The poor women. The church was the only place they could get a little respite from their unending round of chores, and now, wouldn't you know, England has found a way to put them to work there too.

Rome:

The Rabbis and the Rainbow

As the crow flies, Saint Peter's is only a few hundred yards from the synagogue, a massive, square, leaden gray building situated right on the opposite bank of the Tiber. But not until John Paul II crossed the Tiber to visit the chief rabbi had the crow ever flown that route. It was a rarer event than crossing the Rubicon had been in an earlier day in Rome's long history. To tell the truth, I don't think any pope, outside of Saint Peter himself, had ever been seen in a synagogue. It had not been long since the personification of the religion of the synagogue had been painted in Christian iconography as a woman wearing a blindfold over her eyes; moreover, if any iconographers ever knew who had first tied on the blindfold, they certainly weren't telling. It would be stretching a point to suppose that the woman had blindfolded herself to show her determination to be "It" forever in an eternal game of blindman's buff. Could God have been the one who blindfolded her? Or might it not more probably have been the Christians themselves, to keep her from seeing their innumerable sins of infidelity to divine charity?

The Council of Rabbis pronounced their discussions amicable and worthwhile, in spite of the fact that one of them felt obliged to give a speech recounting the long years of humiliation inflicted upon the Jews of Rome, as if the Pope had come there to try to make them forget all about those things—he certainly had no such intention. The chief rabbi's attitude was not so bitter; indeed, he took a very high-minded approach. All the Pope was anxious to do, as he himself said, was to show by his presence there that the Church recognized in Israel the elder brother of Christian people in the order of revelation.

The Pope and the chief rabbi sat in identical armchairs. They did not sit facing each other as in an official business meeting or as if they were meeting in a railway compartment. Nor were their chairs placed side by side facing the audience as if for a debate where the two speakers would be competing for the audience's approval. The two men were seated at an oblique angle, as if they had been two ships, one with a white sail and one with a striped spinnaker, coming in from different ports far over the sea after weathering many a storm, making for their berths in the same harbor.

During the ceremonial visit, there was a torrential rainstorm. A man who had come out to stand on the opposite bank of the Tiber to see what was going on noticed a rainbow arching over the city of Rome.

That kind of atmospheric phenomenon never lasts very long, though. A huge, ink-black cloud soon came to darken the sky and blot out the rainbow: it was the business about Kurt Waldheim, that the media used to whip up a campaign richer in ill will than in cavil. Rarely had an orchestra composed of such fine virtuosos played so many sour notes. A cardinal, carried away by this display, publicly deplored John Paul II's acceptance of the Austrian President's request for an audience, and told the world "how much it hurt him personally", evidently unaware that he was at that moment hurting the Holy Father personally. A winner of the Nobel Peace Prize went on the warpath and accused John Paul II of covering up Nazi war crimes. The memorable synagogue meeting lost its luster as the Holy Father's noble bearing when he walked among the rabbis of Rome faded from the media's memory, and a professor in the University of Bologna even took it upon himself to write that the meeting with Waldheim had "cast a shadow of doubt over the Pope's real intentions". This statement definitely cast a shadow of doubt over the professor's judgment.

We certainly do want war criminals brought to justice; still, like all criminals, they are entitled to due process, and those who prosecute them ought to have them arrested and arraigned before the court where all charges can be made according to law, with proper evidence to substantiate the accusations. When the Pope granted this particular audience, the only available evidence was that some items were missing from Waldheim's file: facts relating to what he did while in the military service. A distressing omission, of course, and one that did look suspicious. But did it constitute proof of guilt? Where was the hard evidence needed to make a conviction? Besides, although popes are not supposed to act as statesmen, they do exercise a power no secular leader can boast: the power to bind and to loose. From that it follows that they cannot refuse to see anyone who makes an official request; refusal of an audience that has been sought through acceptable channels would be the moral equivalent of excommunication.

Be all that as it may, John Paul II is not one to look for excuses for his every act. He considers that he was duty-bound, as Pope and as a priest, to do what he did. All he could have done to avoid such an audience as the one under discussion, he admits, was to have postponed it.

Another sore point between Jews and Catholics had been festering for quite a while: it concerned the Carmelite Monastery that was to be established at Auschwitz. Setting up an enclosure for contemplative prayer within the walls of the most sinister cloister in all history was a generous and perfectly Christian gesture; still, it might have been a good idea to discuss it first with the people who were still so very sensitive about their unwritten property rights to the site of their martyrdom. While it is true that the Jews were not the only ones to be put to death there, they were indeed the only ones to be executed with their babies still in their arms, if the babies were not first snatched from them to be cast alive into the ovens, the modern mouth of Moloch (see Dt 12:31; 1 Kings 11:5, 7). Thus it seems that for the Jews, Auschwitz was not just an accursed plot on the face of the earth, but worse, a pit so monstrous that it might yet swallow the whole universe, a mouth of hell so horrid that anyone standing at its edge and looking down inside is speechless with abomination; they sometimes say that prayer is an impossibility in that place. In their eyes, Auschwitz is a crater more hostile to human life than one on the moon would be, for to them that sink hole abides, emitting a constant, pervasive odor of their children's burning flesh. This was something that should have been understood before the monastery was sited there. Later on, it did become clear to everyone concerned, and the monastery is to be relocated farther away.

Rome:

Theology and Justice

The Pope's theological encyclicals, on redemption, mercy, or the Holy Spirit, have been less widely read, anyway less discussed, than his encyclicals on social issues or his latest apostolic letter "On the Dignity of Women", that spells out his position regarding persistent accusations of misogyny being leveled at the Church, notwithstanding the fact that the gospel begins with a woman called Mary and ends with another woman, called Mary Magdalen, announcing the Resurrection.

There were those who claimed that the Pope dismissed liberalism and collectivism as two sides of the same coin. Not quite correct. His criticism of collectivism's track record over the past ten years is radical:

> No social group, for example a political party, has the right to usurp the role of unique arbiter of social policy, because doing that entails destroying the true personality both of society at large and of its individual members within a nation, the same thing that happens when any form of totalitarianism gains control. In such a situation, both the individual and the people as a whole become "objects" despite all protestations and declarations to the contrary.

For the Pope, such a system is much more difficult to reform than any other: it cannot allow the smallest amount of "leeway", that is, the least bit of freedom, because it is set up like a clockwork mechanism that can fly into fragments if even the tiniest cog works loose.

"If I seemed to come down hard on liberalism," he says, "it is because liberalism is 'easier to fix' than collectivism. However, capitalism also has mechanical defects that keep it from creating a just society."

And what he means by the word "just" is: "The Left counterbalances capitalism. Capitalist countries are only provisional defenders of human rights; if they have done well as far as recognition of workers' rights is concerned, they owe it to the Left."

In practice, capitalist nations are not really in favor of social justice. Their entrenched social structures have roots that reach all the way back to the Roman Empire.

> Where there is imperialism, there is a chance people are going to be treated as slaves. If you have nine rich countries, you have a hundred and fifty poor ones, mostly below the poverty line. Some African tribal chieftains told me recently: "After decolonization, we are in a sense still just as much exploited as we were before." The system was easier to maintain in former times. It is more difficult today because people need each other. Underdeveloped countries have to export their best resources, and if those resources are exhausted, the rich will be the ones who must be held accountable.

In Latin America, people are prisoners of their currency. The money supply has its own laws, and people have to submit to those laws in order to survive. The Pope says: "The cash economy is as totalitarian as any other."

Both systems are equally at fault. You might as well say both systems are equally "in a state of sin" against humanity. One system worships the tin gods of pragmatic materialism, while the other bows down before the idols of ideological materialism. Man's deepest aspirations and man's transcendence are both pushed aside, when they are not prohibited under penalty of law. Neither system would be capable of building a just society, even if it were willing to try. Liberalism leaves initiative to the individual, but at the same time traps him in a catch-22 of conflicts of interest; the political Left claims to free man from enslavement to capitalism, but liberates him only to shut him up again in a collectivist work camp: the results it produces are no better than the ones the liberal system gets.

> Collectivism cannot build a just society. The principle of private property is indispensable. Saint Thomas Aquinas knew that. A man who owns nothing cannot better himself. Who knows? Perhaps *perestroika* will help us all to understand what the thirteenth century meant by the word truth. . . .

Could this be one of those surprises of history John Paul II talks about?

The Pope bases his concept of a "just society", as he does the rest of his philosophy, on revelation, on that affinity that has existed between the human being and his creator from the beginning of the world. As I listened to him, I thought of the New Jerusalem, that the Apocalypse depicts as coming down from heaven, "without spot or wrinkle" (Rev 21:2–4). New Jerusalems that rise from this earth, devoid of respect for the image of God imprinted on all men, are just further variations of the Tower of Babel.

Castel Gandolfo:

"History Is Full of Surprises"

"Holy Father, I happened to be introduced to M. Zbigniew Brzezinski, President Carter's former advisor. We talked no more than five minutes, but what he said in that brief conversation demoralized me for the next six weeks. He told me that according to the most carefully calculated forecasts, in the year 2010 the most powerful country in the world would still be the United States, the second most powerful would be China, the third Japan, and the fourth the USSR. The experts were leaving Europe out of the running entirely since in their judgment it was never going to achieve any appreciable political unity. What depressed me most was that he was not basing this projection on anything but material criteria, economic power, trade, gross national product, currency, and so forth. He added that the Far East would make an increasing impact on the West, and that it was not impossible that by 2020 the United States could have a Chinese President: by that time, the islands in the Pacific would be serving as what gardeners call 'Japanese stepping-stones'."

John Paul II does not think too much confidence need be placed in the apparent logic of history:

> History is full of surprises. Who could have predicted the antagonism between China and Russia, which have grown so far apart today? Nobody could have foreseen the student revolt of May 1968. After that, one might have supposed that

the faithful would be led astray in the confusion. Not at all. Instead they are seeking out the Pope.

He falls silent for a moment, and then adds: "Even their own bishops."

I fought back the urge to suggest that they weren't always finding what they sought.

> Paul VI used to deplore what looked like the weakening and imminent collapse of Catholic Action. But then the *Foccolari* movements, the "neo-catechumenate", and several other movements sprang up, demonstrating that the erosion of spiritual life is not irremediable, and that the Spirit is at work in our midst.

And what of Russia? Do *perestroika* and *glasnost* fit in with his concept of those "surprises of history"?

It seemed to me that the Pope felt a need to take time to weigh the words he would use in his answer: "Gorbachev's whole problem", he says, "is to find a way to change *the system* without changing *systems.*"

Washington:

Truth and Error

Every time the Pope goes on one of his pastoral visits, some bold woman, nun or not, offers her services to teach him religion. There is no way of knowing who delegates these loquacious ladies, whether it is their convents, their diocesan authorities, or whether they just deputize themselves, but the fact is, as soon as they open their mouths, they act as if they had some mandate for so doing. They explain the meaning of life to a man who has undergone, since childhood, enough horrible experiences to break anyone else; they lecture on social justice to a skilled factory worker of long experience; and they preach militant Christianity to a victim who forgave his murderer just as soon as he himself came out of the waters of death. They discourse upon twentieth-century political science to a Pole subjected to two totalitarian governments in succession. They define the priestly state to one who is a priest. They add to those prefatory remarks their own gratuitous agenda of changes they think should be made in the structure of the Church or amendments they would like to see tacked onto the moral code, and they plead the cause of women's liberation in the presence of a supremely loyal son of the gospel who prays to Mary the whole time he is listening to what they have to say.

In Washington, one importunate female activist in particular surpassed even herself in such a rhetoric of redundancy and progressivist mind games that one would have been convinced she had been born, reared and educated entirely in the cafés around Saint-Germain-des-Prés, and that she had studied theology under Marguerite Duras.

A short time after that, *Time* magazine telephoned me to ask me what I thought about the progress of "historical criticism" in the United States. If historical criticism is a brand-new discovery in America, it is not a novel idea in Europe. As far as I know, it can be traced to Spinoza, who suggested as far back as the seventeenth century that the Scripture ought to be subjected to a necessarily rationalistic critical examination. I wanted to know if American Catholics had decided to take the celebrated pantheist lens grinder for their patron saint. *Time* said No, that in the American context the sole purpose of historical criticism was to show, and ultimately to prove, that the Gospels were written down for teaching purposes a good while after the events they recount actually happened, so as to transmit Christian doctrine in imagery that could be easily grasped by average people of that time, obviously rough folks whose minds would have been incapable of understanding ways of speaking other than their own. In short, the Gospels are cautionary tales, fables. I answered *Time*'s question with another question: if the Gospels do not record historical facts, although they claim to do so, then the Church Fathers are all liars and the mystics and saints are all liars together with them, or else they are all the biggest confederacy of dunces history has ever assembled in the name of a single religion. But there is more: If the Gospels are fables written for second-generation Christians, on what basis were the first Christians converted? What initially could have happened to bring such a large number of believers to Christ so quickly, especially considering that Nero was already burning martyrs by the thousands in Rome only thirty years after Jesus finished his course here on earth? What did the apostles say to the crowds before the fables were invented? *Time* did not know anything about that.

I told the Pope how astonished I was to see so many Christians adopting a method based on the mutterings of a pantheist philosopher that would only demythologize their miracles, spoil their feasts, and wreck their faith.

His unruffled answer was to the effect that Americans are very nice people, but when it comes to matters of religion, they have the habit of following, at a sometimes considerable distance, whatever trends Europe sets. Thus it is that they have not yet "got past Bultmann", that German theologian from the first half of this century whose exegesis of the Gospels either plundered them as a salvage diver would a sunken hulk or else skinned them, cut them up, boiled them down, and rendered them into tallow with all the respect a knacker shows a dead cow. In the end, the only thing to do is to have patience; what can't be cured must be endured.

More than once I have had occasion to marvel at the Holy Father's unswerving confidence in the power of truth to resolve things like this more or less by itself. One day, I quoted to him, without citing a book or an author, the trendy new theological catch phrase concocted to posit that "the consecrated bread" in the Mass "was and was not bread, was and was not the Body of Christ", an innovative idea immediately lauded by pencil pushers who found such a liturgical three-card trick utterly delightful for its shock value alone. Next, I sarcastically suggested, they would be changing the canon of the Mass so that priests would have to say: "This is, and is not, My Body . . ."

He answered, "Just leave that error to destroy itself."

Some days, I find, he is *too* good.

Paris:

Designer-Religion

One privilege that France has jealously guarded, left over from her former days of glory, is the right to set the styles in the women's fashion boutiques, and in the "religion boutiques" that might as well be next door to the couturiers', since both establishments seem to be subject to the same extremes of change. Parisian haute couture, as far as I know, puts out two new collections every year, each just prior to the beginning of the season; religious haute couture barely manages to exhibit its new lines by the time the season is over, and has the tendency to show its winter models the following spring; but that's not the only difference.

Fashion designers in the Faubourg Saint-Honoré can dress women to look like blossoms, or beetles, or cones of swirled cotton candy; it doesn't much matter, since the amazing feminine quality of adaptability can adjust to wearing any and all of these disguises. The religious couturier is less ambitious and not nearly so successful; while his colleague is cutting cloth in a studio, he is snipping away at the mannequin herself. I mean he is recutting and redesigning the Christian person to bring her up-to-date, except that up-to-date is only up-to-yesterday's-date; he is always so outmoded and out-of-season that none of his "creations" can ever be called an "original".

He starts with a simple concept, striving for a goal that is just beyond reach.

The simple concept is that traditional Christianity came to an end with the Second Vatican Council, assuming Vatican II was a *pastoral* and not a *doctrinal* council; so the religious fashion designer leaps to the conclusion that there is no such thing as doctrine any more, or that from Vatican II on, doctrine becomes a matter of individual creativity.

His goal that lies just beyond his grasp is to tailor Christianity to fit "modern values", or to piece modern values into Christianity (it amounts to the same thing). The trouble is, the first premise of modernity is that there *are* no values, no values at all, only options and opinions. There isn't much point in trying to cut down a void, or to sew in a vacuum.

The religious couturier is out of luck. Just when he thinks he has it all together, modernity has already changed again. No sooner does he become an evolutionist than certain American evolutionists let it be known that, after all, mankind could have descended from a pair of First Parents, and it is not at all unseemly for them to have been called Adam and Eve; no sooner does he embrace Marxism so devoutly that it becomes, for him, a dogma, than Gorbachev starts to wonder whether the best way to be a Marxist might not be to forget all about Marx when one needs to in order to be realistic; no sooner does he deny that there is a next life than the most advanced findings in physics, the sort of discoveries that win Nobel Prizes, indicate that an *implied universe* exists, and that the world we live in, if I understand correctly, is only a dim copy of the one implied. The designer of religious fashions discovers humanism five centuries after the Renaissance, charges off to storm the Bastille two hundred years after it was demolished, and tries to hire Ernest Renan to write his catechism books, to make sure they are in line with "historical criticism". He names as prophets all intrepid freethinkers who are no more than one hundred fifty years behind the times.

The Pope is too nice a person to use this kind of language, but what must he be thinking when, alluding to Christians caught up in the frantic struggle to take hold of an age that is getting away from them, he deplores the fact that "the Church is being prevented from playing out her role as a sign of contradiction"?

I ask you, what century has ever needed contradicting as much as our own?

Was Christ's Cross a symbol of acquiescence to "modern values", or was it the most terrible sign of contradiction of them all? The Cross flatly rejects the foolishness the world calls wisdom; the Cross stands for the very faith, hope, and love that its superficial appearance would deny.

"We must never", John Paul II says to me, "separate ourselves from the Cross." Driving the point home, he says it again: "Never."

Rome:

"The Word Is Also a Mystery"

I did not tell the Pope what I had heard the previous Sunday in a church in Paris. A lady who had been designated to read the prayer intentions for the week asked us for a special prayer "that the Pope become more conscious every day that Christ is right there with him", a really "caring" thought for the Holy Father's benefit, seeing he was unfortunate enough to live too far from the parish to know what was going on.

I did, however, tell him about what that Mass had been like, with its interminable Liturgy of the Word that reminded me of books whose authors pile up Forewords, Prefaces, and Introductions before ever getting to their subject matter, so that their text ends up accounting for two pages in the Table of Contents. There was a smidgen of gentle reproof in his reply. He pointed out that when all was said and done, although I had taken the back way, I had come all the way 'round to agreeing with Bishop Lefebvre.

As for me personally, I thought maybe Bishop Lefebvre wasn't always absolutely wrong about everything. He was obnoxious when he attacked the Pope on whose very authority his whole philosophical system rested, but at least his recalcitrance may have kept a few innovative tinkerers from carrying their liturgical experiments using faithful parishioners as human guinea pigs too far. In that respect, he probably deserved the tag "user-friendly". The new Mass had been plunked down on ordinary Christians with incredible abruptness, and the more they claimed they were treating us as adults, the more they made us feel we were being treated like children. I, for one, was converted in the days of the old Mass, and I can remember how awed it made me feel. But I am too aware of how much I owe the Church to permit myself to disparage the new Mass even a little. If I had been converted the day before yesterday, I wouldn't know anything but Paul VI's Mass, and I am sure I would feel the same amount of gratitude. I cannot be a traditionalist, because I was not raised in the Christian tradition. In my family, tradition was visits to Père-Lachaise Cemetery and to the memorial to those who fought on the side of the Paris Commune; tradition meant marching in mass demonstrations and sporting the sweetbrier in my lapel before it was supplanted by the rose as the emblem of the French Left.

"Holy Father," I said, "I'm not asking for a return to the old Mass. I just find that the new one isn't as contemplative. It has too much talk and a lot less mystery."

"The Word is also a mystery", answered the Pope.

Rome:

Nonconfrontation and Contempt

In France, the controversy was raging between the progressivists and the conservatives. But it was a new kind of controversy whose antagonists condemned each other without ever squaring off face to face. It was a most amazing thing to a convert like me. I was used to the political confrontations of former times, not to this new way of carrying on a debate where neither side speaks to the other side at all. Instead, both parties cast anathemas down on their adversaries from the safety of the pinnacles of their ivory towers, while their opponents holler their lungs out at the edges of the moats below, and everyone above affects not to be listening. As far as the progressivist was concerned, the conservative had been washed downstream by history's swift current: Was there any valid reason remaining nowadays to justify his existence? To the conservative, the progressivist already had one foot in hell: there was no reason to bother pulling him back by his other foot.

In my whole life, I had never seen Christians look at one another with such contempt.

But John Paul II has a horror of infighting, and he will not have the words "Left" and "Right" used of the Church in his presence.

"That is not the way", he says, "to serve the truth."

However, he did ask me, "What, exactly, is a French conservative?" I answered: "Holy Father, a French conservative is a man who always does the Will of God, whether God wants him to or not."

Rome:

Prelates and Prodigals

We rarely discussed Bishop Lefebvre and the dissident faction headquartered at Écône, Switzerland. It is difficult for a convert born outside the Church to meddle in a quarrel begun by traditionalism. What does he know of the psychological makeup of the kind of people the Anglo-Saxons call "cradle Catholics"? I never used the Church as an object for contemplation, and it even seems to me that the Church is going through this crisis precisely because she has overindulged in introspection, making minute examinations of her structure and subjecting herself to a type of psychoanalysis that can promote only increased doubt and worry.

The Church was made to contemplate God and not her own person. Besides, by the day of my conversion I had learned that the Church was instituted by God and consequently could not be circumscribed by man; no one ever could walk all about her and tell her towers as the psalmist could do in the earthly Zion, and no one could pinpoint where she began or where she would end. I had come to believe that she brought together in herself every gift of God's love that has come down from him from the beginning of time, and that even now she was almost wholly clad in eternal light; we saw only a puny part of her immensity, the part of her that walks with us through the mud here below. I considered it foolish to study her as one would a human institution, for no human institution can be comparable to her, and nothing could be more absurd than to tell us—as we so often have been told—that she had "missed the point of the Renaissance" or the point of the French Revolution, or even worse, that she ought to "open herself to the world"—never mind that she has always been so open to the world that it has worked its way into her shoe and galled her foot like a cocklebur.

Both the progressivists and the traditionalists, as I have said, have committed the same sin: fixing their gaze on the earthly aspect of the Church, rather than on God. The progressivists have made a list of the wrongs she has done, have pointed out her weaknesses and whatever else separates her from the current age and makes contemporary life unintelligible to her or renders her unequal to her task. It is necessary, they think, to adapt her to new times, to teach her to speak the language men speak today, skipping mystery and miracle the better to be relevant to history, sociology, and ethics, so as to present the world with a religion that is as rational as she can make it, regardless of the obvious drawback that a rational religion makes God unknowable. For if reason can tell us that God exists, and I am not at all sure reason has ever succeeded in proving otherwise, still reason cannot by herself explain to us who God is; only revelation can tell us that. And, tragically, for us an unknowable God soon ceases to be a personal God.

Conservatives, on the other hand, fearing they might be contaminated by atheism, frightened by changes in the world, have taken refuge in their doctrinal fortress, condemning anybody who tries to break out. Having reduced the Church to her structure and her rules, their attitude is something like that of Jews hidebound in the law confronting the liberty of Christ. Supposing conservatives had existed in New Testament times: they would have been scandalized, as the Pharisees were, by the episode of Jesus talking at Jacob's Well with the Samaritan woman, one who was cut off from Judaism both racially and morally as a Samaritan and a concubine. Conservatives would have been similarly nonplused by the revolutionary assertion that "the Law is made for man, not man for the Law" (see Mk 2:27; Gal 3:15–19. If he had been there then to hear those words, Bishop Lefebvre would have started preaching about modernism.

The progressivists' thought prompts them by its own brand of logic to make the Church into a kind of political party that calls itself the party of the poor (the honorable choice) but consigns the rest of society either to the dustbins of oblivion or at best to the ramshackle lean-to where history stores its rejects and castoffs. The inconvenient thing about this attitude is that it makes Christianity more of an ideology than a religion: it requires total commitment along with total responsibility, so that baptism gets postponed as if it were a matter of furnishing God with fully trained Christian soldiers marching as to war. Anybody with the slightest practical experience of how God works can see that, on the contrary, God suffers the little children to come into the Church and charges her with bringing them up in the Faith.

The traditionalists are just the opposite. While they cower, walled up in their obstinacy, the twin errors of progressivism and conservatism nourish each other more than they do the truth. The overwhelming majority of Catholics remain faithful to the Pope without allying themselves with either camp. But the progressivists have just as extensive an "old-boys" network as the E.N.A.[1] has in the civil service, and that network has taken over the media, so that the other faction, deprived of the means to make itself heard, has withdrawn farther and farther into itself and

[1] Ecole nationale d'administration.

turned semicatatonic. Bishop Lefebvre became a Le Pen[2] for the conservative opposition, with the result that a number of the followers of the Bishop from Écône can now be found in the ranks of the National Front.

As far back as 1975, the saintly Father Journet, who would have preferred not to be made a cardinal but accepted the red hat as a matter of obedience, predicted in a letter to a nun that Bishop Lefebvre's fractiousness would inevitably bring about a schism.

> My dear Sister, [he wrote], I am very much alarmed by what you have written to me. People see a drift toward the heresy of modernism, so they create a countercurrent flowing straight into a conservative schism. Here comes another Port-Royal to tear France apart, and not just France alone, but the whole Church. And this new Port-Royal is a much more formidable model than its prototype, because if these conservatives try to justify their schism, they will be obliged to see heresies in the Pope's decisions and in those of an ecumenical council. . . .

Amazingly clairvoyant. The prophecy was fulfilled thirteen years later, despite the forbearance of John Paul II, who, patiently enduring the insolence and clumsy accusations of a refractory bishop who was entirely too sure of himself, made offer after offer of reconciliation and issued invitation after invitation that would have eased his restoration to full communion. Bishop Lefebvre opened his door and listened, but only so that he could immediately close himself off again with a resounding slam. As Father Journet had prophesied, the Bishop taxed the Pope and the Council

[2] Philippe Le Pen was the head of a nationalistic party in France. High unemployment had led to feelings of animosity against foreigners. This resulted in an emergence of the extreme right wing and the formation of this party, which won 11% of the vote in the 1984 European elections.

with heresy and illustrated by his impertinence that there are none so blind as those that will not see, insinuating that John Paul II was inciting revolutionary activity when as everyone well knew, the Holy Father tirelessly preached nothing but the kind of justice that stops revolutions before they start. Eschewing confrontation, Bishop Lefebvre barricaded himself behind a wall of inconsistencies: while insisting he was a traditionalist, he bent every effort to loosen the keystone of Tradition itself, undermining the principle that the Church depends on the Chief of the Apostles. While opposing freedom of religion, he took advantage of the privilege in the basest possible way, aligning himself squarely against Rome; advocating order, he provoked disorder. He was a priest long experienced in making his own confession and hearing those of his people: now, he couldn't even identify the temptation to spiritual pride if it were to walk up and greet him by name, and it was a temptation as tremendous and as glittering as the peaks all around Écône, something that was going to induce him to set himself up as the final authority on what was good and what was bad for the Christian community.

Until he could do no more, John Paul II expended himself to stop Bishop Lefebvre or at least slow him down in his headlong race toward secession, and on several occasions one would have thought the Pope's efforts were meeting with success. Unfortunately, the Bishop acquiesced on one point only to refuse to budge on the next, and, if he behaved more amenably in private, he forsook all decorum once he got out in front of a crowd again. However, at the beginning of May 1988, it looked as though he might be starting to soften up. Yet, it is when negotiations are closest to succeeding that the risk of failing is greatest: Bishop Lefebvre signed an agreement with Rome on May 5, and reneged on it the next day by announcing his intention to consecrate four bishops on June 30. This was an unmistakable threat of schism, not just a break in diplomatic relations but a theological rift besides, and therein lies the thing that is hardest to grasp about this man who was as much throttled by the law as the learned doctors of the temple were in Jesus' time.

Clearly, the tie that binds Christians to one another and to the pope in Christ's Church is not at all similar to the type of linkage that splices together the members of some party or interest group; it is infinitely stronger than that, and it has a name. It is called the Holy Spirit. No platform or common cause can make Christian souls children of God. It takes a Person, the third Person of the Trinity; the logic of the Faith defines every attack on unity as amounting to the same thing as grieving, indeed wounding, the Holy Spirit; speaking metaphorically, to make schism is to cut off one of his wings.

On June 29, an hour before midnight, the Pope's last offer arrived by telegraph at Écône. John Paul II urged Bishop Lefebvre in moving words to cancel the consecration ceremonies scheduled for the following morning that were sure to sever the Bishop from communion with the Catholic Church.

But Bishop Lefebvre already had his butcher knife in his hand.

Conservatives, before the schism, certainly had more than one tenable excuse for being upset. It is true that those magic words invoking "the spirit of the Council" had encouraged such liturgical and doctrinal curvettes and airs above the ground that the *aggiornamento* John XXIII envisioned sometimes seemed more like a cavalry charge than like the slow march of progress. The "cradle Catholics" no longer quite knew what their religion was all about, and confronted with priests who seemed to be treating them like slow-witted missing links whose evolution as a species had come to a standstill, Catholics who had been born Catholic felt vaguely guilty that they still believed what they had been taught when they were children. Reforms, some justifiable and some less so, were foisted on them with no warning and no preparatory instruction. Sadly they watched as the curtain went down for the last time on their childhood vision of a heaven peopled with shining angels with golden wings, and they even had to stand by quietly, their faces pale with dismay, while the demythologizers took out all the wonder of the Bible stories their parents had read them at bedtime, and the liturgical demolition squads had at the intricate carvings and polychrome with axes and hammers. They were coming rapidly to the conclusion that John XXIII had been just as imprudent to convoke Vatican II as Louis XVI had been to assemble the Estates General. Those were the days when Paul VI was talking about the Church "self-destructing". Traditionalists thought they could save the Church by setting themselves against all modifications, be they interior or exterior, the same way people pass city ordinances prohibiting modernization of historic buildings.

But even if the traditionalists were not always all wrong, it does not follow that they were all always right. They did not perceive that Vatican II had freed Catholics from the Jansenist pessimism that had made religion a chore for three centuries, an attitude that turned the faithful into dour pilgrims, eternally guilty, marching fearfully toward salvation while ignoring the beauty of creation. The outside world was a place of perdition, and by opening herself to that world, the Church of the Council was doing nothing but making herself vulnerable to temptation and sin. On the other side, the progressivists greeted the advent of the liberal Church with jubilation. They took it into their heads that

Vatican II had given them license to toss all the furniture out the windows; their intention was to become wedded to their times—but "marry in haste, repent at leisure". Espousing one's age is a dangerous project because time is a coquette who never tires of burying her lovers.

And so, on her outermost extremes, the Church was torn between an evolutionist Left that did not believe in original sin and a far Right that correspondingly did not believe in redemption. While the Left was busy breaking with the past, the Right bragged that it embodied the epitome of Tradition, when all it actually had succeeded in embodying was Port-Royal.

Bishop Lefebvre's rightist faction, of its own free will, went ahead and excommunicated itself on June 30. Still chanting its amaranthine slogan "*Extra Ecclesiam, Nulla Salus*" (Outside the Church there is no salvation), it took hold of the doorknob, opened the door, went outside, locked the door behind it, and swore up and down that it was the one that was still *in* while everybody else was *out*.

In the course of this medieval morality play, you could see some of the characters defending the virtue of faith portrayed as political philosophy of the rightmost fringe, garbed in every thread of narrow-mindedness and bigotry. Other characters took the part of the virtue of hope, in the guise of statistical projections that rested primarily on the promises of history. But of course, history is always making promises and never keeps a single one. What about charity, the third theological virtue that stands as the foundation of Christian behavior and distinguishes Christianity from all the other religions? I never caught Bishop Lefebvre practicing it, for he was immobilized, stuffed into his too-tight suit of doctrinal armor studded with anathemas, no more capable of flexibility than those unhorsed knights who could move no more than an arm's length in their rigid brassards and cuisses and who could see only the handbreadth of world visible through their visor slits.

I didn't see charity being practiced, either, by those who called the ones who eventually defected from Écône "penitents", an epithet Italian courts use to designate terrorist informants who denounce their fellow gang-members to the authorities. I found no charity in the prelate who declared himself willing to help "those who recanted", as if, in the parable of the Prodigal Son, the father had granted his forgiveness subject to his son's signature on a written act of submission. In the parable, the father simply rejoices at his son's return and kills the fatted calf, without requiring any sort of formal ceremony before the feast. How generous that Gospel is, how superbly loving! It ought to be read out loud in all the churches. But the Bishop never said anything about a fatted calf. All he offered his returning prodigals was permission to kiss his foot.

Where was any charity in this vocabulary of intolerance and interdict? Charity consists in freely forgiving offenses, in loving one's neighbor, someone who for a Catholic may be merely another Catholic who is trying to preserve the Church's oneness, a unity mirroring the Unity of one Divine Person. Charity dwells in gentleness and great-heartedness. Charity lives in John Paul II—and it is what the schism has wounded in him.

Rome:

Uncle André's Way of the Cross

The youthful masters of ceremonies at the Vatican are sergeants at arms and courtiers entrusted with preserving the noble grandeur of ritual at Saint Peter's. Without them, pontifical ceremonies would be disorganized, haphazard liturgical jumbles with cardinals walking in circles and bumping into one another. These young experts know the rubrics backward and forward, when to sit, when to stand, when to process around the altar, when to put on the miter, when to take it off, when to direct the choirs to sing, and when to stop the music. They tactfully and unobtrusively indicate the pope's place in the book and they move with silent, stately steps from one corner of the *sagrato* (pavement, area around the altar) to the other, attired in their elegant royal purple robes with never a pleat too many, steepling their fingertips beneath their chins like donors of holy pictures in days of yore. But the 20/20 vision emanating from under their downcast eyelids misses nothing whatsoever, and, be their hands never so piously joined, the index fingers of their right hands, possessed of singular alacrity and a will all their own, move instantly to straighten anything out of place or to beckon to attention the server whose mind may be wandering, or, by subtly describing a minute circle, to let an acolyte know it is time to turn a square corner and go back to his place.

One fine January morning, it occurred to these extraordinary young men, who affectionately referred to me as "Uncle André", to ask me to compose the exhortations for the Stations of the Cross that the Pope would celebrate on Good Friday at the Colosseum. They cleared this matter with their warden, Monsignor Magee, who in turn told Don Stanislas, who then consulted the Pope. The Holy Father gave his consent to their plan and confirmed it with me the following morning. It was the first time ever that a French writer, and a layman to boot, had been invited to write the Way of the Cross for the celebration at the Colosseum. It was going to be broadcast on television to all the Catholic countries *except* my own.

Badgastein:

"Christ Can Inspire Anyone, Even a Writer"

The little resort village of Badgastein, bolted neatly and securely onto the sides of rough Alpine crags, retains an old-fashioned, faded elegance from its heyday, when it was one of Austria's popular spas. It even had the honor, from time to time, to be a vacation spot favored by the imperial family. If you made Vichy a good bit smaller and put it into a funnel, it would look like Badgastein. A *wasserfall* runs through the middle of the town, a rushing cataract that descends at regular steps down the mountainside, its boiling rapids sending up clouds of spray as it plunges downward making a noise like the sudden flushing of a water-closet. Our hotel, situated at some distance from the center of the village, squatted between a freight-railway siding and some warehouses. Here, where nobody spoke a word of French, I came to grips with the fact that I didn't remember a word of my four years of high-school German, not even the few syllables of patois I had picked up from some of my Alsatian relatives. The skies were gray, everything was covered with snow, and the only way to get to town was to slip and slide over a vertically sloping, very icy, and narrow road. I had only one thing on my mind: work. That Way of the Cross had to be written, and I had exactly three weeks to do it. But Christ can inspire anyone, even a writer.

Many Christians, intimidated by the posthumous triumph

of the goddess of reason, prefer to pass over the miracles in the Gospels in silence. But I once met a bold preacher who had a wrestling match every year with the angel of the Annunciation. The man just could not believe that the Virgin Mary could have received a message from an angel. What must have happened to her on that day could only have been that she gradually became fully aware of the nature of her mission; all the rest was pious claptrap. Another preacher held that the miracle at the marriage at Cana was only an allegory, a prefiguration of baptism: I suppose that is how, after Jesus had changed water into wine, the commentators got up the nerve to pummel the text until the wine changed back into water. There is no need to elaborate on the unfortunate sunstroke that converted Saint Paul to Christianity on the road to Damascus. It is obvious that the amazing fellow who figured that out had halogen on the brain, so that his head was as light as the headlights of the same name. If Christians keep on shoving miracles back into the landscape of legend, they will soon discover that they have sent God off to never-never land right along with them.

Somehow, these putative Christians do not seem to be able to deal with the realization that the Gospel is miracle through and through, the miracle of a Presence outside of time, a Presence who never stops asking us, from the first line of the Gospel to the last, that question of questions Peter was asked three times over: "Do you love me?" (Jn 21:15–17). As I wrote these Stations of the Cross, I felt again the power of this strange Book, leading from when Jesus is condemned to death to when Jesus is laid in the tomb, reaching its culmination when the One who called himself the "Son of Man" dies on the Cross. And I wrote, "O Christ, thou diest that we die alone no more." Faith teaches us that the one Person of the Savior is known in two natures, human and divine. In a sense, we also have a human nature and a divine nature. But our divine nature is revealed in our suffering, whereas Christ's human nature is known in his.

I finished my writing in Salzburg, a city as lovely as an Austrian Verona, at a round table in the saloon bar of a hotel so small that you could not get in or out the door without bumping into the furniture. Then I left for Rome to submit my text to the Holy Father (it met with his approval). There was a coating of snow two centimeters deep on the streets, the trains did not dare come all the way into the main railway station for fear of skidding, and the citizens of Rome were rattling around in cars fitted with tire chains, since nobody there ever thinks of getting snow tires. One of the morning papers came out with the headline: "The Snow Is Falling, The City Is Holding Her Own".

The Colosseum:

Recollection You Can Reach out and Touch

Every Good Friday in Rome, the Colosseum is lit up on the inside by a number of circular rows of kerosene torches, or *fiaccole*, that cause the tragic monument to take on the appearance of a giant incinerator. The spectacle of these little orange-colored lights that are used only for funeral processions the rest of the year is one of melancholy beauty, but no one got to see it: after the Pope came out of the amphitheater, the huge arena stayed empty all night long. Outside, however, thousands of the faithful were reading the little book of the Stations by the light of candles stuck into cones of paper; the candlelight glancing off the books made it look as if the Way of the Cross were lined with an infinite number of human faces.

At nine p.m., the Pope stepped out of one of the gates like a martyr raised from the dead (they say no Christians were actually martyred in the Colosseum, but they also say Shakespeare never existed). After a short prayer, he would speak no more until the final homily at the fourteenth Station on the Palatine Hill, a dark Golgotha where one can dimly see the broken columns of a ruined pagan temple, where the music of the lyre that once hymned the antique gods is now forever stilled. At the first Station, the Pope, carrying a wooden cross in front of him that was large enough to be used for its original purpose, took a few steps forward, stopped, and a voice rang out in the night. His recollection was so profound that one felt one could reach out and touch it: the Passion is the central point of all his teaching, the gateway to the global view of history that marks his whole philosophy. Once, he spoke to me with sorrow about "the conformist, secularist mentality" that is developing in the Church, leading her off the track laid down by revelation, and turning many people away from the Cross of Christ.

John Paul II carried that cross from Station to Station in a manner showing it to be the Church's greatest blessing; and it is true: the day the Church forgets that Cross will be the day Christianity comes to an end.

The Pope at prayer, Auschwitz.

Auschwitz:

A New Definition of Martyrdom

It was the Holy Father's personal wish that Maximilian Kolbe be declared a martyr and canonized as such in October 1979. All the consultants at the Vatican were against it. It was all right with them to have his name inscribed in the catalogue of "Confessors of the Faith", the title given to average, run-of-the-mill saints. But martyr? They cited for the benefit of those who supported his cause the traditional definition: "A martyr is one who testifies to the Faith, even unto death inflicted as an act of hatred of the Faith."

Maximilian Kolbe was a Polish Franciscan born just before the turn of the century. He was in poor health (he had only one lung), and he was consecrated to the Virgin Mary with a devotion whence he seemed to draw all of the incredible amount of energy that enabled him to found, in just a few years, an enormous publishing enterprise and the largest Franciscan community in the world (it sheltered and provided work for six hundred friars). Maximilian Kolbe was deported to Auschwitz by the Gestapo, who refused to forgive him for declining the German citizenship that was his by right, since he had a German-sounding surname. And at Auschwitz one summer day in 1940, he stepped out of a column of prisoners to take the place of a man who was the father of a family, a man who had been condemned along with nine other detainees to wait in a bunker, without food or water, until an escaped prisoner was recaptured (an unlikely prospect); in other words, the man had been sentenced to die of starvation. After twelve to fourteen days of unremitting agony, Maximilian Kolbe, who had survived his fellow sufferers, was executed by a lethal injection of phenol.

The consultants in the process of canonization did not, certainly, deny the beauty of what Maximilian Kolbe had done. It was an act of heroism, surely; and who would have denied that it was also an act of charity? But where was the martyrdom? It lacked at least two out of the three elements required in the definition. Had he been brought to trial for his faith? Had anyone said to him, as they used to in the good old days of Nero's and Domitian's persecutions, "Deny your God, or die"? No. Had he been killed "in hatred of the Faith"? The consultants could not find the slightest trace of that kind of hatred in his executioners, but those same consultants could not see that it was there all the time, at the heart of the Nazi system, a pagan system ("conscience"—and therefore the commandments of God—was, according to Hitler, "an invention of the Jews"), a totalitarian system that put any dissident exactly in the situation of the early Christian who would not pinch incense to Caesar's divinity. At the end of the chain, the more recent tyrant (Hitler) was merely bringing this hatred that was central in the early days of persecution to its pragmatic conclusion. However, another consultant came along to encourage the Pope to go ahead with his plans: since the Faith is bound up with love, an act of charity is also an act of faith. If the Pope had ever hesitated, he held back no longer. Maximilian Kolbe would be venerated as a saint and as a martyr. In addition, Saint Maximilian Kolbe had, without knowing it, himself provided a new definition of martyrdom when he wrote in his little Mass intention notebook: "*Pro amore, usque ad mortem*", "For love, even unto death".

John Paul II's decision had far-reaching influence. It made necessary a reworking of the classical definition so as to include a sweeping condemnation of totalitarian regimes, not limited to their pernicious ideologies alone—as in the period since Pius XI—but dealing for the first time in no uncertain terms with "martyrogenic" systems. Moreover, if a dissident's disinclination to obey such a regime leads to his death, he is indeed a martyr in the religious sense of the word. "Then, for that reason alone", I said to John Paul II one day when we were discussing Maximilian Kolbe, the first saint canonized during his pontificate, "the last war, taken all by itself, produced millions of martyrs we can pray to in any church anywhere in the world".

He nodded his head, and looked at me with an expression that said, as plainly as if he had spoken the words aloud: Why not?

Rome:

Imperishable Images

I tried repeatedly to coax the Holy Father to take a trip to Ravenna. This bright spot, its mosaics dispelling the barbaric shadows of the Dark Ages of the fifth century, offered sanctuary like a restful glade that never failed to refresh after many a mental and spiritual scramble up and down our century's miry tracks; Ravenna was my refuge from all the insolence and shocking conduct that mar everyday twentieth-century living. These icons, gently and brilliantly expressing the Faith of the early days of the Church, fitted in quite naturally with John Paul II's personality, for he had been steeped from his youth in that kind of faith, as his native Poland had been, in the Byzantine school and in the Roman school, too. Christianity today is highly moral, certainly, and highly prone to moralizing, but it lacks some of the freshness that enchants the visitor to Ravenna, and it seemed to me that the Pope would derive comfort from contemplating these images created from precious, imperishable minerals. There are some people naïve enough to call Ravenna's icons naïve, albeit the holy images epitomize the highest form of art and religious thought of all time. The Holy Father had been there when he was young, so he did not have a very vivid memory of it; but it would hardly have been possible for him to go back again, since, as he reminded me, he had very little time to devote to tourism, no matter how educational an excursion might be. His trips are arranged at least a year in advance and his travels require so many preparations that once they are fixed on his calendar, it is nearly as hard to reschedule them as it would be to shift the moon from its orbit and make it revolve around the planet Mars.

However, I was not ready to throw in the sponge just yet. Several months later, I made the suggestion again. Since he was kind enough to ask me if I was going to Ravenna for my vacation this year as usual, I answered that over the past twenty years or more it would never have occurred to me to spend my holiday anywhere else, and I told him that I always felt my spirits lift when I got to the point on the Ancona highway about twenty kilometers out of Bologna where the green arrow with large white lettering indicated the exit for my personal corner of paradise. I thought I might tempt him by saying that one could find there, in the message in the mosaic work that no one has ever quite deciphered, a view of history as powerfully original as his own. But he did not seem excited about rereading his own philosophy, so my second try failed as miserably as my first.

My third attempt was considerably more successful. I must let it be known right away that, unbeknownst to me, my third suggestion coincided perfectly with an official invitation he received from Emilia-Romagna, and messengers were going back and forth between the Vatican and the dioceses of the Emilia-Romagna region all the while I was being my most persuasive self, pointing out to the Holy Father that Ravenna was not just mosaics, but that one could also go there to inspect refineries, factories, a tanker port that would surely become tomorrow's Rotterdam on the Adriatic, and that besides the saints of the early Church both male and female and the angels in heaven, all the town's hundred thousand inhabitants would turn out in force to welcome him. Everything was already more than halfway arranged. The Pope was going to take his trip to Emilia and to Romagna. I was to be there too, not in a very important capacity of course, but I was invited just the same. The Archbishop promised that between having lunch with the nuns and the big rally at the district stadium, I would have two hours to take the Holy Father to see a few of the sights. The Archbishop was very busy with the pastoral part of the visit, but he knew how to be flexible.

Ravenna:

An Icon among the Icons

When the Pope arrived at Ravenna, I had been an honorary citizen of the town for three months to the day: I owed this honor to a unanimous vote of the townspeople and to their communist Mayor. As everyone knows all too well, Italian communists are more intelligent than any other kind. His Honor the Mayor had admitted me to honorary citizenship with a very spiritual speech that the Archbishop rounded out with a friendly, down-to-earth talk; both men were roundly applauded. To my honorary citizenship I owed the joy of being allowed to guide the Holy Father through the city whose very walls shine with pride that their town contains the most valuable treasury of permanent souvenirs from the springtime of the Christian Faith, and the saints who lived there a millennium ago and now dwelt in the City of God seemed to be still very much alive, rubbing shoulders quite naturally with us as we walked together through the same luminous, imperishable garden. It was the barbaric night of the Dark Ages that had dug the fatal gulf that made heaven look farther and farther above our heads, and it was in those bad old days that the world had turned into this "valley of tears" whence we even now send up our sighs, mourning and weeping.

I told the Pope I had always felt like a native of Ravenna because it was there that I found the tangible image most like the imageless image I had seen on the day of my conversion: the compact, sparkling world in the mosaics was a near-perfect replica of the spiritual universe, made concrete, with no visible empty spaces, the universe that had become for me absolute reality, the sort of reality that admits of no further questions.

He pointed out that I had exactly reversed the normal order of sensory perception, and I had no trouble seeing his point. Then he asked several questions that I was able to answer with the help of a walking "dictionary" of Byzantine art whom I had taken the precaution of bringing along: Don Montanari, an expert in early Christian symbolism. The Holy Father was much taken with the joyous message on the walls in San Apollinario *Nuovo*, where, in a riot of brilliant colors, the holy images refute the alleged "antifeminism" in the Church once and for all: on the wall at the left of the nave, the virgin-martyrs and holy women, all properly canonized, do not seem to be suffering any male-chauvinist insults from the bishops, confessors, and Doctors on the wall facing them, and the Virgin Mary, wearing her crown and sitting on a throne on the same level with her Son's, is surrounded by the same heavenly host.

The next morning, the Pope celebrated Mass at the Church of Saint Apollinarius *in Classe* (the Mariners' Church), the ancient parish church built to serve the port but well inland now that the coastline has become more built-up. Vested in a chasuble of cloth-of-gold and a gold-brocaded miter, he might have been either a mosaic that had detached itself from the wall or else a mosaic about to make itself part of the wall. After Mass, he went to bless the wedding of the sea to the little port of Cervia in a launch loaded to the gunwales with monsignori who held tight to the sides of the boat with one hand while using their other hands to keep their birettas from flying off their heads into the water. As tradition dictates, he threw the sea's gold wedding ring down toward the water, but it never even touched the waves of the Adriatic: a waiting swimmer treading water below caught it in midair. I wondered if the sea would consider this grounds for an annulment. That evening, he boarded the motorcoach to go back to his helicopter. He leaned out from the platform as the bus pulled off, bidding everyone goodbye and waving profusely and affectionately at the crowd. I stayed behind on the beach with my awestruck communist aediles and His Grace the Archbishop, who was no less impressed, and the crowd, who looked as if they all felt young again.

Cervia:

A Candid Snapshot of Faith at Work

The Holy Father is the kind of physical specimen that fitness experts would call a "man of steel". The day he became Pope, when he went out in front of the crowds for the first time, his white cassock and broad shoulders leaving a broad wake behind him and his face glowing with health from being out on the steppes in the sun and wind, he gave an impression of incredible strength: he was like the heavy, ironclad cruiser Potemkin steaming into harbor at Saint Peter's, like a cavalry troop suspended in midcharge, or like a hurricane harnessed. And it is true that there are some untamed, redoubtable aspects to his personality, perceptible in the almost furtive rapidity of some of his gestures, his sometimes catlike tread: you don't hear him coming up behind you unless he chooses to announce his arrival by putting one of his mountain-man's feet down hard. He is a lion from the peaceable kingdom, but a lion all the same, and anyone who thinks he can take advantage of his gentle mien had better think twice about what could happen to the foolish person if the lion were to lash out with a paw—something he'd never do, of course. At the table, he often sits beside you so that his "good ear" is toward you (he doesn't hear quite as well since he was shot), and the keen look in his eyes (gray, blue, or green, depending on the light), passes over you without staring to go on to fix on a morsel of bread or some other inanimate object that has the quality of letting his thoughts run unchecked. When he speaks French, Italian, or any language other than his own, his subtle Slavic accent gives his voice a unique charm. You think you may be hearing the crashing of waves, or the buzzing of bees, or an echo of a brass choir from a long-ago Easter festival. His clean-shaven, unblemished countenance, photographed more than any other pope's face has ever been, keeps its own counsel. No film has ever been made that is sensitive enough to take a candid snapshot of faith as it accomplishes its work in him.

Pope John Paul II and the Lech Walesa Family.

Warsaw:

A Union Man among Union Men

While he was on his third trip to Poland, the Pope made the rounds of the whole territory of social issues and didn't miss a thing. In season and out of season, he spoke the forbidden word "Solidarity", a word that takes only four syllables in Polish to convey the hopes and aspirations an entire nation will never abandon, and at every opportunity he called the government to account and recalled it to its duty with regard to human rights and the dignity of the individual human being. Did he sense any flagging spirits, any discouragement among the workers in Poland? It looked as if he might have been trying to rekindle hopes half-stifled by the repressive countertactics the regime in power used so arbitrarily, as if more and more buckets of ashes could smother the light in a common man's eyes when he is dreaming of being free again one day. He spoke as a union man to union men, as well as as a pope, and he said everything Lech Walesa, that admirable worker-statesman, was not permitted to say with impunity. He exalted Solidarity's ideal, which he said was valid not just for Poland but for the whole world, for Western democracies in particular. That ideal, in a nutshell, is to make huge, impersonal corporations into companies, societies, where *people* matter more than profits.

He could not have gone further without provoking hostilities, and one could tell by the authorities' mute agitation that they were worried about something that simply was never going to happen. Their tension kept on increasing, and General Jaruzelski could not stop himself from letting John Paul II know what he thought of him, in a statement that barely concealed his contempt, during the private meeting he had with the Pope at the airport on the (blessed) day of his departure. The General complained that the Pope had treated the government with greater severity than usual: "No, I didn't", said John Paul II with a smile. "All I did was to quote you your own Constitution."

Communist governments never remember that what they have written in their constitutions is the opposite of the things they actually do.

Montreal:

Defending the Faith in Canada

I was invited to speak at the Catholic University in Montreal. When I arrived, I was welcomed by a professor of Church history who was a native of a village near the one where my grandparents grew up. He was a Lutheran pastor. I jokingly asked him how it could have happened that a fearful heretic was the one chosen to guard the doors of a papist university.

"My dear compatriot," he answered, "you should thank heaven I'm here to defend sound Catholic doctrine. If it weren't for me, you have no idea what they might be teaching these nice people", he added as he introduced a gaggle of coeds who had been waiting, notebooks in hand, to hear my lecture.

We progressed from being compatriots to being good friends in no time. I recalled for him Montesquieu's prediction that by the time Montesquieu had been dead two hundred years, all the Catholics would have turned into Protestants.

"They already have," chimed my jolly Lutheran, "and now they are all so Protestant that it's discouraging Protestants from becoming Catholics."

And in fact, while I was being interviewed on a Catholic television broadcast, I was required to answer the trickiest series of criticisms and objections toward John Paul II that had ever been put to me. In summary, they went something like this:

"Why is the Pope opposed to priests being married?"

"Well, if you want to get married you have to be your own person, and a priest is not his own person. A priest belongs to Christ. So ask Christ."

"When the Pope was in Washington, a nun made some strong criticisms of him. Did you hear what she said to the Pope?"

"*That woman* . . ."

"What do you mean, '*that woman*'? She was a nun."

"Are you sure she was a nun? John Paul II was orphaned quite young. By the time he was twenty, none of his relatives were still alive. He went through World War II working for the underground, he was a factory worker for several years. He and his fellow Poles endured Stalin's purges, and he suffered just as much as every one of them did. Tell me something about what your woman, excuse me, I should have said your nun, went through, and I'll see if I think what she said when she tried explaining to the Pope what life is all about is worth listening to."

"Why does he refuse to allow women to be ordained to the priesthood?"

"It is not he, but the Catholic Church. Unless I am sadly mistaken, you belong to the Catholic Church, don't you?"

"That doesn't answer the question."

"Well then, as far as I can see, the principal function of a priest is to say Mass, to 'reactualize' the sacrifice on Calvary. Now, as for women, they never had anything but a helping, kindhearted role to play in Christ's life. No woman ever betrayed him, and no woman ever had any part in condemning him to torture and death. It is appropriate, then, that it should be men who re-present that shedding of blood, since no woman ever had anything to do with it. Why do you want women to break the Host, and in so doing, break the Body they never delivered up?"

"How do you explain the fact that the Pope, who is so liberal on social issues, is so far behind on the subject of morality in marriage?"

"Whom is he behind? Just the people who think that the new morality means having no morals at all?"

It went on in that vein, touching on artificial contraception, abortion, Bishop Marcinkus, and Vatican finances. When it was over, I felt a little depressed, so I sought out a priest.

"Sir," he said, "the Church of Canada has been too strict for several centuries, and so now the same thing has happened to her as happened to those dirigibles with rigid frames that the least shock or spark could cause to burst into flames. I feel sure the spark was set off by the May 1968 student revolt, but the canvas skin of the airship had already suffered quite a few scuffs and punctures since the war."

So, when the Pope got to Canada in the next few months, would he find the Canadian church going down in flames like the Hindenburg? I was pleasantly surprised, I can tell you, when he got there; Canada indeed caught fire, but with admiration for him.

What a beautiful country! I toured some of her gorgeous expanses of white snow and blue sky, lit by a powerful transfiguring light that made the icicles on the fir trees sparkle like diamonds and made the man who pumped gasoline into my car look as glorious as Moses and Abraham on Mount Tabor. Going down the Saint Lawrence, a river that flows upward toward its source, pushed along by the swift tide, I looked at the horizon and saw a long white line that I thought was a whitecap on a wave: it was a flock of thousands of wild birds resting before migrating to sunny California for the winter, like the aristocratic ladies of long ago who fluttered from Baden-Baden to Monte Carlo or from Montreux to Spa, according to the season. I met a few optimistic priests, who were enthusiastically getting ready for the Pope's visit, a few bishops, and perplexed or concerned faithful, who did not feel very reassured after reading the newspapers that vied with one another in criticism before the fact and well-bred scepticism.

Some cloistered nuns received me in their enclosure, and the arrangements they had made for entertaining me knocked me flat. Imagine, if you can, in the middle of a large, unfurnished room, a sort of pen made of narrow wooden latticework with openings just large enough to look through or smile through, but not big enough to do both at the same time. The nuns were waiting for me inside this cage, clumped together like wise, silent birds, and making no noise other than the sound of rustling, wimpling wings. They admired John Paul II, so we understood each other very well. They offered me the joy that came forth from their pure souls, along with a little bucket of maple syrup, and I went my way feeling much refreshed, to visit their neighbors the Trappist monks who gave me just as glad a welcome, but without the cage. The monks knew how much Christians today owe John Paul II, and they saw clearly that religion in their country was going through a crisis that could hardly be dismissed as growing pains. The best way to understand the world is not to immerse oneself in it, but to stand outside it. Contemplatives, enclosed in their monasteries, seem fully occupied with an invisible universe far away from day-to-day realities, but they are much more difficult to fool than actives, who are decidedly prone to running after mirages.

The Ursuline nuns in Québec took me to visit the tomb of Marie de l'Incarnation, whom they considered to have founded their country with the help of Saint François de Laval. He was canonized, but she has not been canonized yet, although this great mystic's reputation extends over the length and breadth of three centuries. The Ursulines made me promise to get involved in helping to put her case before the congregation in charge of causes for canonization of saints, and they also begged me to ask the Holy Father to visit their convent. I agreed to do everything they asked: one does not say No to Marie de l'Incarnation, the glory of France—and the glory of the Church.

Some laywomen who had become involved in various apostolates invited me to a dinner, and they briefed me on the role of women in the Church in general and on women in the priesthood in particular, in about the same language as was used by the Catholic television interviewers. My argument based on the love women had shown Christ at his Passion was to no avail. I tried another tack, suggesting that, anyway, the priest's job could not be targeted for affirmative action, and that candidates for the priesthood were not exercising a right but trying to fulfill a vocation, and the two things are not the same. It was not the priest who had chosen God, but God who chose the priest, and the day it pleased God to have women fulfill the office of priests, it would be God who took care of making his Will known to the Pope. But that argument, too, suffered the Hindenburg's fate. Nothing I said would do; it was the principle of the thing. They couldn't, they told me, accept being prohibited from being ordained, even if as individuals they had no desire to become priests. They did not, however, deprive me of my dessert, in consideration of the efforts I had made to win them over.

Professional observers of the religious scene set to work to throw water on the joy I had derived from visiting the nuns in their cage, the Trappists, and the Ursulines. They told me that the Pope's pilgrimage was not getting very good publicity; that Canadians were little by little adopting an American life style, concerning themselves with political economy, sociology, and history; that you couldn't talk to Canadians and pretend Freud never published a book; that I would have trouble finding Christians of my own ilk in the Far North, that Christians in Canada were made in the image of the city of Montreal, whose skyscrapers extended not only into the skies but down into the earth through several stories of subbasements housing shopping malls and mercantile enterprises of all kinds: and that that explained why Canadians, even when they are looking up toward heaven, are continuing to do business deals down in the subbasement of their subconscious. In short, the Canada of today was no longer the Canada of Marie de l'Incarnation or of A. Frossard. The Pope would not be understood; he might even, perhaps, be politely refuted.

A few friends tried to comfort me as best they could, insisting that their fellow Canadians had changed less than they claimed to have changed, and I departed from Québec in a very ambivalent state of mind, vacillating between optimism and anxiety. It is one thing to write about the Pope in a newspaper and quite another to look him in the eye.

When I got back to Rome, I kept the promises I had made to the Ursulines. I believe in the extremely important role mystics play in the life of a nation, I believe that the world of tomorrow, if it still asks itself questions, will go to the mystics to find answers from these singular beings who have experiential knowledge of how God operates. It is no inconsequential matter that there is at least one mystic, and often several very great mystics whom one can consult, in every country in the world. The twenty-first century would profit by listening to what Marie de l'Incarnation said in the seventeenth century; souls like hers stand outside of time. So I marched off to find out where she stood with the congregation for causes of canonization, the keepers of the register of the elect. I entered into the presence of the eminent personage who was willing to receive me with that brand of Roman diplomacy that suffers the Tiber to run between the parties in a conversation to keep everything on an impersonal basis, and I explained my amazement that Marie, who had been beatified long ago, had not yet been canonized and that this situation was keeping her from getting the official recognition she deserved in the diocese of Québec.

"Well," answered the eminent personage, "we're still waiting for her second miracle. Did you by any chance bring any miracles of hers with you when you returned from Canada?"

"I never thought about it. But why on earth do you need a miracle from a lady who had regular conversations with the Holy Trinity? Isn't that miracle enough?"

"Ah," said the circumspect personage, "she could have just been missing a few of her marbles."

The Church treats mystics with a certain amount of mistrust, and she always will. Nothing embarrasses the Church so much as unexpected manifestations of what she still sometimes refers to as the "supernatural", because for those who learn about God by methods other than faith, the "supernatural" is only this material world, with its own mysteries, its odd way of perduring in being, its atomic structure, its black holes, and its component changes and chances. Disappointed, I went to seek courage and consolation from the Holy Father. I did not dare ask him, right that minute, for a halo for Marie de l'Incarnation, but I was sure that if he went to the Ursuline Convent in Québec and stayed there for a while it would only require a minute's visit to a certain black marble tomb that I never looked upon while I was there without feeling strong emotion, to give a healthy boost to the cause I had agreed to champion, with or without a miracle. He told me that the stop was on the schedule and that he would certainly go there.[1] Then, I told him all about my trip, and I had yet another occasion to observe how discouraging signals have a way of increasing his enthusiasm tremendously. The way he works is to place his duties in the framework of prayer and turn himself and everything else over to God. The word "abandonment" comes up often in his books, and it is this abandonment that keeps him from ever giving up.

For my part, I thought, and if I remember correctly he thought too, that as far as this trip was concerned, everything depended on the first ten minutes.

And what a triumph those first ten minutes on Canadian soil were. Two hundred thousand Québécois were there to greet him, singing a lovesong from their traditional folk repertory, and the wave of enthusiasm blew as if driven by hurricane-force gales, all the way across the country to Vancouver.

Some weeks later I returned to Canada. It was Indian summer, and before the onset of winter, nature was putting on a farewell performance in her costume of gold, purple, and black velvet. The Canadians seemed to me to have attained unanimity. Wherever the Pope went, religion took on new

[1] He never made it. An overworked organizer in Québec made the mistake of telling him that Marie de l'Incarnation's tomb was a long distance from the city (it was two hundred yards away from where he was at the time), and there was a crowd waiting outside to see him besides.

life. With simple, ingenuous joy they discovered that they had never stopped being Christians, and their clergy, who had been knocking themselves out for years trying to speak to their people in a new language, were stupefied to find that the Pope was no longer using that kind of talk. One excellent bishop confessed to me that he was surprised to see this unprecedented flowering of Christianity. He had been dazzled, as I was, by the way the Canadian forests can hold the sun in their dense branches and almost postpone the sunset. I thought it over carefully, and then devoutly vowed to do everything in my power to make our wonder at what was happening in Canada last longer than that Indian summer.

The Pope blesses the people.

Journeys:

Peter, Paul, and John Paul II

It was calculated that the Pope had already traveled, in kilometers, the distance from the earth to the moon and halfway back again. Taking into account the advances in modes of transportation and the difference in speed between the commercial airliner and the barques the apostles used for their missionary journeys in early Christian history, one may wonder whether this latest pope has done any more traveling than the first one did, bearing in mind as well that Saint Peter's journeys probably engendered the same kind of critical attitudes: "What a waste of money! Why should Peter go to Rome, when he has plenty to do right here in Jerusalem? As for Paul of Tarsus, wouldn't you think he'd have learned his lesson after being shipwrecked three times?"

Only the Pope gets accused of wasting money on his trips. You never hear remarks of that nature being made about the politicians who junket to meetings at the North Pole or the South Pole, just so they can have "meaningful dialogues" that don't amount to a hill of beans, smiling broadly and shaking everybody's hand with vigorous insincerity. Nobody ever points out to them that their meaningless communiqués cost the taxpayers quite a lot, and look how much money that takes away from welfare programs. These folks whom the Pope suddenly inspires to be unwontedly thrifty have a patron in the Gospel, the one who went about in the company of the disciples and took Mary Magdalen to task for spilling three hundred denarii-worth of precious ointment all over Christ's feet (John 12:3–7). That frustrated do-gooder's name was Judas Iscariot.

The Holy Father gets around, but he also takes crowds with him and that becomes another reason for criticizing him. The people who blather on all year long that "the Church must go out into the world" abruptly take it all back when the world comes into the Church. When they claim that they want to "open up the Church", it isn't to encourage the people to come in, but so they can go out for a breath of air, something they hardly need since they are already fully inflated. All they are looking for really is specious publicity and fleeting popularity and the comparisons they use are just as worthless as their currency. They think they know why John Paul II draws crowds, but they really haven't a clue. Crowds follow him because he is the last intermediary between heaven and earth, because he represents the only shred of hope the world has left, because he believes in God and is not afraid to confess his faith before all men, and because they would like to believe the way he does, without hesitation and without reservation. And he goes out to the crowds because his heart naturally prompts him to do it, because he loves his neighbor, because every human being is in his eyes a tabernacle where Christ dwells or a place where the Holy Family may find lodging, since they made it rather obvious when they were in Bethlehem that they knew how to make do with a stable. And he does it for yet another reason, that he explained to me: "God made himself visible in the Incarnation. Therefore the Church also must become visible."

And there is no use in trying to keep him from traveling. Before he went to England, everyone told him what a terrible idea it was to go there. The English are cold; all that fog only makes them more so; their education makes them snobbish; they will be polite, but standoffish. He might not even meet a single person, with the possible exception of his official hosts, who would throw himself into his arms. He paid no attention whatsoever to these dire forecasts. He went, and was welcomed enthusiastically. One might have said that England had been repopulated overnight by Neapolitans. The Pope walked with short, dignified steps and drew precise, tiny crosses in the air when he gave people his blessing. Amid the unexpected warmth of the huge mobs of cheering Anglo-Saxons, he was the only one acting like a Brit.

His pilgrimages knit up, thread by thread, the raveled sleeve of Christianity that in the past had a tendency to come apart at the seams. This is one of the three good deeds he has done for the Church. The second is his clarification of doctrine that he works at without stint, from holding audiences to writing encyclicals, transmitting messages in his apostolic letters, and preaching sermon after sermon: the instructions he gives on Wednesdays week by week make up for the deficiencies in the catechism books. The third good deed is perhaps the most extraordinary. I have already written about it: it is his defense of humanity and human rights.

Paris:

Exorcising the Zeitgeist

One can read some very strange observations about the ten years of his pontificate. For example, an eminently intellectual Catholic publication confides to the reader that it worries about the "universal catechism" that the bishops at the 1985 synod hailed as just what they had been hoping for: "One may well wonder if a universal catechism may not be in fact a sort of iron collar intended to restrain the vitality that Vatican II reinjected into the churches by celebrating a diversity of cultures and life-styles." You could say the same thing about the Creed that they cruelly make people say in the same words in all four corners of the globe, and that abridges dreadfully the rights of freethinkers down through the ages. And here's another one: "It is becoming more and more clear that the Pope is guided by an interpretation of Vatican II that does its best to be a faithful one, although it rests, as far as Christian faith and social action in the Church are concerned, on a doctrinal view that is basically preconciliar." The author does not tell us in what *postconciliar* Christian faith consists, for the very good reason that he knows nothing about it: "In the complexity of a transitional epoch", he says a little further on, "undeniably out of touch with the historical background and thus vulnerable, despite the presence of the Spirit, to uncertainties, tensions, and other worrisome and unpredictable unknowns. . . ."

Obviously a Christian thinker cannot put his trust in anything but his own genius. The instance of the passive presence of the Spirit would be funny if the writer were not deadly serious. So would his final observation: "One may legitimately identify in John Paul II a concern with strengthening the faithful in their sure convictions, in what forms the basis of their faith. This preoccupation on his part was transparently manifest in his Wednesday public audiences." Could this be, by chance, a backhanded compliment? I'm afraid not. "From this point of view, the Pope is placing himself in a situation that differs from that of his immediate predecessors and from that of Vatican II, to the degree that he seems ill-at-ease in this transitional era that opened, for Christianity, with John XXIII." In other words, the immediate "predecessors" of John Paul II were busy with some work other than that of "strengthening the faithful in their convictions". What could they have been doing? Nobody knows. That is the mysterious thing about "transitional eras".

Paris:

Pointing the Way to the City of God

De Gaulle probably would never have returned to power in 1958 if he had not found good old President Coty sitting there in the Élysée Palace weighing the pros and cons of resigning.

Between the reigns of Paul VI and Karol Wojtyla, the ephemeral pontificate of John Paul I was no doubt necessary, and if the premature death of this good pope had not been perceived as a kind of invalidation from on high, perhaps no conclave would ever have broken with tradition in order to elect a Polish pope.

They say that the intellectuals, the newspapers, the politicians, the leftists, and the rightists were all against de Gaulle. The only ones that were for him were the voters.

John Paul II encounters the same obstacles in similar situations, and the only ones that are for him are the faithful.

De Gaulle, shabbily treated by legislative bodies, was, if I may say so, obliged to go over their heads in order to get his ideas across to the people. Hence his frequent recourse to the referendum, with the result that he was criticized, of course, for bypassing the accepted democratic institutions whose purpose is, as everyone knows, to enable the people to express their will as often as possible.

John Paul II, who is no better served by most of those who are supposed to support him in his work, also goes directly to the people, and his pilgrimages come close to being called unauthorized referendums by a certain group of clerics who feel that they are better qualified to interpret the will of the people whom they never see.

De Gaulle always said, "Financial report to follow." John Paul II probably would cheerfully make the same kind of response to people who question him about Vatican finances.

Pride cannot see much farther than the end of its nose. Humility broadens its horizon, and when humility takes on its intellectual form as objectivity, it gives a man that global view of the world that identifies him as a statesman.

The General's thought processes constantly dwelt on what was going on in other parts of the world, and he was in the habit of observing the development of whatever country happened to interest him at the time from different perspectives and altitudes. So it is not all that surprising that sometimes, on coming back to earth from one of his mental aerial world tours, he could make a mistake about where he actually was at the time, and once he cried out "Vive Fécamp!" when he was really in Dieppe.

John Paul II has the same worldwide viewpoint and sometimes thinks simultaneously about the Far East, the West, Latin America, Africa, and Oceania. If he doesn't get mixed up about where he actually is, it is because he takes time every evening when the sun goes down to make sure he knows what country he is in.

On the base of the Cross of Lorraine that stands watch over Colombey-les-Deux-Églises, one can read the inscription: "Humanity is the only thing worth fighting for."

I don't know whether John Paul II knows this saying, but I do believe he would not hesitate to make it his own, although he would replace the word "fighting" with the word "working".

For de Gaulle, France was a spiritual gift of history, and

that concept made all the difference between his nationalism and that of his rightist adversaries.

For John Paul II, every nation has its own special calling, and these vocations proper to each nation make for the unity of all nations and impose duties on each nation toward the others, as well as toward itself. He sometimes addresses countries as if they were people: "France, eldest daughter of the Church, what have you done to fulfill the promises you made at your baptism?"

Having said all that, I do not mean to force parallel lines to intersect. The two men do not have the same background. De Gaulle fought a long war against the darkness that threatens, from age to age, to engulf peoples and civilizations. John Paul II's personal quest will reach its goal in the light of the "new heaven" and the "new earth" of the gospel.

Santiago, Chile:

The Mission to Be Present

Having learned that the Catholic University of Valparaíso had had the idea of making me a professor and the wisdom to add to that title the words *honoris causa* that would excuse me from giving lectures and students from listening to them, the reverend Jesuit Fathers of Santiago had the happy thought of inviting me to lunch.

I was in hopes they would tell me about what was going on in Chile, a country I knew nothing about save what I had been able to see through the airplane window: a long, green strip being pushed toward the ocean by a huge mountain ridge of snowcapped peaks set in an immense empty space. Between the Andes and the Pacific lay a country intended to be a geographical call to contemplation, but one that for a long time had been distracted from her vocation by politics and poverty. After we landed, Santiago affected me as if it had been a giant waiting room. On top of the hill, a white statue of the Virgin Mary awaited the faithful, who in their turn were perhaps waiting for her to come down into the town; everybody was waiting, but what were they waiting for? The next earthquake? The next overthrow of the government? I was sure the Jesuit Fathers would be able to tell me.

There were twelve of us at the table, and each one was perfectly courteous, although slightly distant, as is almost always the case when religious entertain a layman, coming as he does from a breed apart. One of the Fathers asked the blessing in Spanish. It began with the words, "We who are your disciples . . ." In Chile, it is easy to rise to the top, for the mountains are a big help. The superior looked at me pleasantly, but it was a look that had the strange property of making me feel as if I were being moved farther and farther away from the table. I don't remember seeing a smile on a single face among the men around the table, all concentrating on their plates, applying themselves to eating as they applied themselves to scholarship. They ate their lunches as they read their books, to analyze them rather than to enjoy them.

They weren't interested in talking about Chile, but only about the Pope, and my hosts' mind-set filtered down to me across the hors d'oeuvres in the form of questions: "Don't you think, Sir, that the Pope's personality speaks louder than his words and that his presence does more good than his message?"

The father who was speaking to me seemed to come from northern France or Belgium; I don't know why I thought so, maybe because he had the strong, solid appearance and ruddy coloring of a brick building. You could tell he was voicing a generally held opinion, and the sense of what he was saying was clear: the Pope's popularity was a media event, but his ideas did not suit the times and the masses did not really understand him.

I answered: "Reverend Fathers, I do believe that this was also the case with Jesus Christ. When he went up onto the Mount in Galilee to say to the crowd: 'Blessed are the poor, blessed are they that mourn', was he understood by the people who nevertheless remained at his feet and asked him for nothing, not even for bread, since it seems to have been the apostles who first thought of feeding them? When he went on to say that they must eat his flesh and drink his blood to gain eternal life, was his message understood, when we cannot be sure even now that anyone has ever fully deciphered its full meaning? Did he not say, one day, 'My sheep know my voice', and not 'My sheep understand my anthropology'? I wonder if faith is not simply something that comes by hearing, and it seems to me that the Person of Christ 'spoke louder' than his words just as the Holy Father's personality does, and in spite of Jesus' having said so many enigmatic things, they still followed him in procession on Palm Sunday, and spread their garments in the way."

I could have added that even the apostles themselves did not seem to understand a great deal about their Master's sayings and parables: for them, it was enough that he was there, and they did not even ask to know any more about him. They basked in his presence without speaking, as if they were warming themselves in the sun.

However, I cannot thank the Jesuit father from Santiago enough for having spoken as he did. His question helped me to understand something he must have known all about, but that I had never thought of before: Christianity is essentially a religion of *presence*. Its revelation is the revealing of a presence, the Incarnation is a presence, the Eucharist is a presence, and the Pope's mission is to be present.

Castel Gandolfo:

Redeeming Human History

History is something we live day by day with our noses deep in our newspapers, but for the Pope, history is an object of contemplation.

History resembles those Dutch landscapes that seem to be made up more of sky than of land, and in which the land seems to fade into the light in the distance. And just so does the divine economy of redemption govern the world, in that it enfolds and encompasses the world most often without the world's knowing it, and in that it will finally be the world's salvation.

This thought derives its inspiration from the first book of the Bible, that contains everything we need to know about what it means to be human, about the dignity of the human person (made in the image of God, Gen 1:26), about man's vocation ("subdue the earth", ibid.), and about the first, fatal temptation, repeated from age to age ("you shall be as gods", as the serpent promises Eve, Gen 3:5). "Some gods!" the Pope says, "they couldn't even rule the world, and they died besides. . . ." As if lifted up by a hurricane of prophecies, that thought speeds on its way toward the Incarnation, the Cross of Christ, and salvation, while on the horizon rise "the new heaven and the new earth" announced in the good news.

The Holy Father says: "By entering into us, God entered into human history, and divine history came in with him."

Divine history will come to fruition, no matter what sins we commit, whether past, present or future sins, for all things were redeemed on the Cross on Calvary.

Human history comes second—I think he may even have said it was "secondary" in importance. Inevitably and without fail it will resolve itself in divine history, without having had the slightest effect on our freedom.

"Redemption is at the center of my prayer-life", he says. "In it the whole reality of God is revealed to us, both what he meant to be for man's sake, and what he is in himself. It is in redemption that we see that God is love."

Rome:

The Child of the Light

Throughout his entire ten-year reign, he has never allowed himself the luxury of idleness. He reminds me of those Polish workers in Nova Huta, who worked every night to build a wooden church that the authorities had pulled down the following day. The workers did not tire of building and the men in power did not tire of pulling down.

It is the same with John Paul II, as day after day he works to reconstruct the edifice of Christian faith and morals that the world keeps on tearing down day after day. In Nova Huta, the workers finally got the better of the authorities. They have their church. And John Paul II is the same kind of worker as those men in Nova Huta.

The first thing that struck me about him is the amazing unity in his personality. I had already made note of it in *Be Not Afraid!* while we were working closely for months on end: "There is no difference between what he thinks and what he is, what he believes and what he says, and this literally nuclear inner cohesiveness is what makes him glow." He is the same whether he stands on the steps of Saint Peter's or sits across from you at the table, there is not any public John Paul II or private John Paul II—for the reason that he does not have a private life.

He is remarkably attentive to the Will of God, concerned with justice to the point of being scrupulous about it, an enemy of discord; he reverences truth in all its aspects, he bears with injustice toward himself without complaint, and the virtue of hope, that he practices by being obedient to the virtue of faith, corrects any negative conclusions he might reach as soon as he reviews them in the light of his extremely clear reasoning. He has an infinite respect for the sick and for all who suffer; in his eyes, their weakness even confers an immense spiritual power on them, and he thinks they help him to bear the burden he has on his shoulders that would crush anyone else.

His devotion to Mary has nothing affected about it; it is reminiscent of that of Maximilian Kolbe, and it is strong enough to make it possible for him to accept the terrible experience of the attempt on his life as a grace. He loves children, and one of the loveliest pictures from his pontificate is the one of the Pope, wearing his miter and all his most elaborate vestments, walking on the long red carpet down the aisle of Saint Peter's toward the pavement in front of the altar, leading by the hand a little girl who had gotten lost in the crowd, whom he took in his arms and held up as high as his hands would stretch so that her parents could see her and come and find her again. The reason he loves children so much is that he still retains in his heart something of the child who wants to join in their play.

Having said that, he still is not such an easy person to analyze. But when he is sitting at the table, at one of his luncheons that are completely unofficial, where, consequently, it is all right to refrain from speaking without risking giving offense to anyone, the silence allows you to gain a gradual insight into his personality. First of all, you have the Pope sitting across from you, like a great white bird with folded wings; if the silence continues and permits you to go on with your study, you will see, beyond the Pope, the in-

The Pope with a young friend in Mexico.

delible character of the priest; beyond the priest, you will find the man, and the man's fundamental modesty will lead you directly to the child he once was, and from whom he has never been separated and even seems to be still leading along by the hand; after the child, there is nothing but the light of God, that he does not see, but that enlightens us all.

Then you will remember how he told you one day that man was an abyss.

Photographic Credits

cover	Catholic News Service/Joe Rimkus, Jr.
p. 8	Catholic News Service/KNA Photo
p. 14	Catholic News Service/KNA Photo
p. 28	Catholic News Service/KNA Photo
p. 38	Catholic News Service/Arturo Mari
p. 57	Catholic News Service/KNA Photo
p. 62-63	Catholic News Service/KNA Photo
p. 64	Catholic News Service/KNA Photo
p. 94-95	Catholic News Service/Arturo Mari
p. 132	Catholic News Service/KNA Photo
p. 144	Catholic News Service/Arturo Mari
p. 156	Catholic News Service/KNA Photo
p. 172	Catholic News Service/KNA Photo